Seeing Jesus in the Old Testament

HE'S NEVER ABSENT, WE'RE NEVER ALONE

LYSA TERKEURST

AND JOEL MUDDAMALLE

table of contents

LYSA
terkeurst

JOEL
muddamalle

SHAE
tate

leadership

Lisa Allen
Meredith Brock
Melissa Taylor
Kendra LeGrand

project manager:

Victoria J. Smith

editorial:

Glynnis Whitwer
Eric Gagnon
Abbey Espinoza
Kenisha Bethea
Claire Foxx

design:

Tori Danielson

WELCOME

to the study

I didn't want to say it. I didn't want to feel it. I didn't want to be struggling with it. Yet I know it's impossible to fix problems I refuse to admit I have.

"I'm not sure the Lord is really with me."

I was in a season where I'd been doing church for a long time. But I kept having this suspicion that other Christians had a more direct line to God than I had. Things just seemed to work out for them. They kept gratitude journals and had plenty to write on those pages every day. And when we would study the Bible together, they had incredible revelations that they'd express by saying, "These verses really spoke to my heart ... The Lord just showed me something amazing ..." Or, "I see His hand moving so powerfully in my life right now."

I would hear their confidence and want to quietly pack up my notes and Bible, which didn't have nearly the amount of highlight marks in it as theirs did, and just go home. What was I missing?

Sometimes I would feel a rush of assurance and comfort when standing with my hands raised in a crowd electric with praise songs. Or I had a rare moment when something big happened and I could declare, "Wow, look what the Lord did!" But I wasn't like those other girls at Bible study. And I was too afraid to admit my uncertainty to anyone or ask questions.

I just kept quiet. And faked like I had the same unwavering spiritual confidence that everyone else had. All the while, internally, I couldn't shake this nagging thought that if Jesus really cares about me, why does He seem to stay hidden from me? And if Jesus really wants a relationship with me, why can't I see Him, hear Him and get to know Him? I mean, if a human relationship was this mysterious, I'd assume the person was ghosting me, rejecting me and giving me the not-so-subtle hint to move on.

Then I remembered some relationship advice I'd heard: If people want to improve their connections with friends and family, they need to communicate their desires more clearly.

Maybe that's what I needed to do with Jesus. So I wrote in my journal three desires I had for my relationship with Jesus:

1. I want to see You.
2. I want to hear You.
3. I want to know You.

At first, this felt so odd and strange. After all, I knew I wouldn't likely physically see or hear Jesus. But what my heart was crying out for was to see evidence of His reality in my life. I truly wanted to experience His presence and walk in the assurance that He saw me, heard me and wanted to know me.

I KEPT JOURNALING ABOUT THIS *and then one day decided to turn that list into a prayer I would pray each day.*

And eventually I added, "I want to follow hard after You every day so before my feet hit the floor, I say 'yes' to You."

I decided, after praying that prayer each day, that I would start looking for Him with greater intentionality throughout my day. I would tune in to my own life experiences and start living with expectation of this prayer being answered. It's now been over 20 years since I started praying this prayer.

And every part of my life has been dramatically impacted for the good because of learning to practice the presence of Jesus and live with expectation of experiencing Him daily.

I still think about that doubt that haunted me in my early days of following Christ: "I'm not sure the Lord is really with me." I can't say that doubt doesn't ever creep back in my mind. But what has dramatically changed is that doubt doesn't send me spiraling into panic and hopelessness now. I'm not afraid doubt is a sign that my faith is weak. Quite the opposite. I see doubt as an invitation to pursue new strength.

I want to become even more certain that Jesus is near, that He cares, and is still very actively moving in my life.

This past year, a relationship ended that I fought hard to save. I thought this would be the season of us living out a beautiful story of reconciliation. I didn't expect to be back in a pit of heartbreak and disillusionment where nothing made sense and everything hurt. I remember staring at my Bible and wondering: *Where are the answers to my prayers? Where's my miracle? When will I start to see some of the promises of God come to fruition in my life? Jesus, where are You?* And then when I actually opened up my Bible, I felt so tired of dealing with hard circumstances that I didn't have the energy to turn past Genesis.

I kept asking God to help me know with greater assurance, confidence and courage that He was with me. And He did, but in such an unexpected way. As I was reading the first two chapters of Genesis I was reminded of something I needed to remember: God showed me that Jesus is very much mentioned in the creation story.

I always remembered Jesus was prophesied about in the Old Testament, but I forgot He was also active in the first part of the Bible.

And that's when I realized it would be fascinating to do a Bible study on seeing Jesus in the Old Testament. After all, if we can see Jesus in unexpected ways in the Old Testament, maybe that will give us more awareness of His presence in unexpected ways in our lives today. Jesus has never been one to hide. And He's certainly not hiding from us now. We just have to know how He presents Himself so we can see how present He is in every aspect of our lives today.

If you are like me and you've been longing for:

Greater comfort that Jesus is near ...
Greater confidence that Jesus cares ...
Greater courage that we aren't fighting alone ...

Welcome, friend. You're in safe company here. If you've been through some tough realities in your life lately, this is a wonderful Bible study to do right now. Or if you want to better prepare for seasons of hardship with more comfort, confidence and courage, then you're in the right place. And certainly, if you are just fascinated by digging into God's Word with greater depth but in a way that won't make you feel lost or confused, that's a great reason to dive in with this study as well.

Joel and I thought about you all the way through the writing of this study, and we can't wait to share all we've learned with you, together.

Love,

INTRODUCTION *to the study*

In a survival situation, having a compass could be the difference between life and death. Even if you've never found yourself stranded in the woods, desperate for direction, most people know a compass can tell you where north is at all times.

But the benefit of a compass doesn't stop at just telling you where north is. A compass also tells you where north isn't. A compass isn't only a guide; it's also a guardrail.

Wouldn't it be nice to have a compass for everyday life? A tool offering guidance for tough decisions and giving advice when you aren't sure which direction to turn?

A compass could be so helpful when we're studying the Bible. Especially as we navigate the Old Testament. Let's be honest ... some verses and sections of Scripture can feel confusing, complicated and not relatable to our everyday life.

And if it doesn't easily apply to everyday life, it sure feels justifiable to skip over.

But what if we've been overlooking the compass that's been there to guide us through Scripture all along? Jesus *Himself.*

You see, the Old Testament is not just a journey through biblical history before Jesus suddenly arrives in Matthew. Jesus has been present from the very beginning.

John 1:1 gives a crystal-clear clarification that Jesus was present in the Genesis 1-2 creation story. In John 1:1 (ESV) it says, *"In the beginning was the Word, and the Word was with God, and the Word was God."* Verse 14 clarifies even further that *"the Word became flesh and dwelt <u>among us,</u> and we have seen his*

glory, glory as of the only Son from the Father, full of grace and truth" (emphasis added).

Nothing was created without Jesus (John 1:1-14) and everything is perfected by Jesus. We can see Jesus as the one who perfects what humans can only do in part. In the Old Testament, there were three offices of leadership that led the people of God: prophet, priest and king. However, everyone in the Old Testament who held these offices did so imperfectly. The reality of these imperfections created an even deeper anticipation for the promised Messiah who would eventually hold all three offices, but in complete perfection.

It's the truth of Jesus as the Greater Prophet, (Matthew 13:57; Luke 7:16) Priest (Matthew 1:21-23; 1 Timothy 2:5)[1] and King (Matthew 1:1; 9:27; 12:23; 15:22) that gives meaning and understanding to every word, sentence, paragraph and page of the Bible from Genesis to Revelation. And it's the presence of the promised Messiah in the Old Testament that helps us see the brilliant truth and glory of Jesus on display in the New Testament.

Because Jesus is Truth, He is our True North. He is our guide, our context and our example, not just through the Bible but through our lives as well. And if we can discover Him in unexpected ways through the Old Testament, we will realize He didn't just appear mid-story in the New Testament.

If we were going to watch a movie today, we wouldn't start in the middle. We'd miss so much context to what makes the ending so profound by skipping over the beginning.

The same is true for how we read our Bibles and experience Jesus through reading Scripture. If we want a more complete understanding of who Jesus is to us and how He keeps us pointed in the right direction, we need to read the full story of Scripture. And if we want to be comforted by the assurance of His presence, seeing how He makes His presence known in the Old Testament will help us more clearly discern His presence in our day-to-day life right now.

Jesus is never absent in the story of the Bible, and He's certainly not absent in any part of our story either.

When we start to see Jesus in the Old Testament, our eyes are opened. Our hearts begin to long for the fulfillment of God's promises to restore, reunite and redeem His creation. Jesus is the center of this redemption story. Jesus is the compass that shows us the way.

Jesus is the guide to help us see the great story of God throughout all the pages of Scripture.

In fact, the entire Old Testament testifies to the promise, presence, protection and proclamation of the peace that Jesus provides. And aren't we most desperate for this kind of assurance when our future seems unclear, our prayers seem to go unanswered and more unexpected heartbreaks make us want to doubt?

Is Jesus actually there? Yes, He is.

Does He actually care? Yes, He does.

Sometimes when we get lost in our brokenness, we need the Bible to show us our perspective is limited. What we see isn't the full story. And the way things are right now won't be this way forever.

Lysa here. I wish we were sitting in my den right now so I could take your hand and look you in the eyes with all the tenderness that's in my heart right now. I wish I could hear your story. And I wish you could hear mine. I would assure you that, while this study is deep, it will also be clear about the ways these truths apply to our lives right now. This study isn't to just give our minds more knowledge. It's to give our shaky hearts more assurance and confidence that Jesus has always been and will forever be with us. And not just with us but actively helping us.

SEEING JESUS IN THE OLD TESTAMENT *THROUGH* PORTRAITS *PROPHECIES* PATTERNS *PROVISIONS* *PROTECTIONS*

So we pray this study takes you on a journey over the next five weeks of pausing to look for Jesus through some surprising places in the Old Testament, including:

1. PORTRAITS

We can see partial glimpses of Jesus through people in the Bible, as we understand who they were and what they did to help paint the picture of the coming Messiah. These individuals prepared the way for Jesus and partially fulfilled the expectations that He would later completely fulfill.

2. PROPHECIES

We can see Jesus through the prophecies that tell of Him coming in the flesh. It was foretold that Jesus would be the King who would not only bring justice but ultimately right all wrongs.

3. PATTERNS

We can see Jesus in the patterns (and opposites) in the Bible like famine and rain, or wilderness and promised land. These help us connect the ups and downs of life to the consistent reality of the presence of Jesus. He Himself represents a pattern of both the suffering servant and the reigning King.

4. PROVISIONS

We can see Jesus providing physically, emotionally and spiritually for the people of the Old Testament. For example, the Israelites needed to be cared for and led during their 40 years in the desert before entering the promised land. In the same way, with Jesus, we are not left lost, wandering and helpless. He Himself is our perfect portion and provision.

5. PROTECTIONS

We can see Jesus through God's actions throughout Scripture to protect His people. As we study, we'll start to discover the ultimate protection we have in Christ Jesus. Even when we feel scared, undefended and uncertain, we can be confident that Jesus hasn't abandoned His role as our protector.

Never have we needed these reminders more than right now. We are so grateful to take this journey alongside you as we encounter Jesus like never before.

-Lysa and Joel

"IN THE BEGINNING, God created the heavens *and* the earth."

GENESIS 1:1

"In the beginning was the Word, and the Word was with God, and THE WORD WAS GOD." JOHN 1:1

"The earth was *without* form and void, and darkness was over the face of the deep. And the SPIRIT OF GOD was hovering over the face of the waters." GENESIS 1:2

"He was in the BEGINNING *with* God." JOHN 1:2

"And God said, '*Let there be light,*' and there was light." GENESIS 1:3

"ALL THINGS were made through him, and *without* him was not any thing made that was made." JOHN 1:3

"And God saw that THE LIGHT was good. And God *separated* the light from the darkness." GENESIS 1:4

"IN HIM was life, and the life was *the light* of men." JOHN 1:4

"God called the light Day, *and the* darkness he called Night. And there was evening and there was morning, the first day." GENESIS 1:5

"The LIGHT SHINES in the darkness, and the darkness *has not* overcome it." JOHN 1:5

WEEK
one

1

SEEING JESUS IN THE OLD TESTAMENT
THROUGH PORTRAITS

Have you ever woken up to a glorious sunrise and felt mesmerized by the array of colors stretching across the sky?

Lysa here. I will often say to myself, "God painted that just for us to see this morning. I wonder how many will notice His stunning artwork today?"

Or have you ever encountered a painting that grabbed your attention and you couldn't just walk past it? It might have been beautiful, but more than that, it spoke to something deep down inside of you ... compelling you to stare in amazement.

An artist has an inspired desire when they dare to pick up brushes and dip them into the paint. The shapes, colors and images are all intended to elicit a response. And unlike a photograph, which can only capture what's in front of the lens, the painter gets to create the scene, arrange the colors, set the mood and intertwine their personal message with every stroke.

When we write these studies, we relate to painters so very much. Only we use words (and theology) rather than brushes to evoke emotion, tell God's story, find our place in His story, and invite the reader to learn from God's wisdom and our collective experiences.

Throughout Scripture we find constant word-portraits that the Master Artist Himself placed in order to remind us of His presence. And the portraits that God presents in Genesis through Revelation are like shadows revealing the presence of Jesus.

In a painting there can be hints contained within the artist's work pointing to a bigger picture or message. The same is true with God's Word. There are shadows included in God's story that, if we see them, point to a bigger message inside the story. These shadows reveal the reality that Jesus is there.

Physically speaking, shadows prove the sun is shining. The sun shines and creates a shadow confirming someone or something is standing in the light. So the shadow is evidence of light and the physical presence of a person or object. But shadows aren't as detailed as the real person or object. Shadows give us a shape but not a complete picture.

Spiritually speaking, the portrait-shadows we find in the Old Testament lead us to proof of the presence of the Son. There are many shadows of Jesus in the Old Testament, including portraits of people who reflect versions and variations of Jesus. But just like physical shadows, these "shadows of Jesus" give shape or partial reflection of who Jesus is but never a complete picture of Him.

Bible scholars have a technical term for what we are describing; they refer to this type of study as "typology." Essentially, each of these portraits paints a "type" of Jesus, and understanding these "types" helps us to see the purpose and work of Jesus in clarity and fulfillment in the New Testament.

We will trace the history of God's people throughout the Old Testament and find that Adam, Eve, Moses, Joshua, David and Esther are all shadows or portraits that point to Jesus. Though they were imperfect with human flaws and frailties, each of these figures in Scripture, at times, did good works in their assignments. In that good, we find glimpses of a greater good that Jesus would eventually bring and complete. Each glimpse shows how Jesus will eventually right the wrongs and reveal His radiance as the light behind every shadow because He is the Son of God.

As we study five different portraits pointing us to Jesus, we will find these individuals have a common experience: God meets them in the most unexpected places. In the very moments they want to give up and quit, the nearness of God's presence gives them the courage and strength to take their next step forward.

Friend, maybe you, too, have your own moments of feeling like the only solution is to throw up your arms and call it quits:

.... when you get an unexpected phone call that shocks you with heartbreaking news.
... when you reach a dead end in a dream that feels like it's never going to flourish.
... when you've prayed for change in a difficult relationship that just isn't getting better.

We so deeply understand.

But we also know, in that very moment, the presence of Jesus will give you the same courage and strength to take your next step forward, too. It doesn't even have to be a big step. But we can live with the confidence that Jesus is already there, meeting us in all the angst and fear we feel.

As you study these portraits in the coming week, we pray the affections of your heart are stirred for the One who is even greater.

THE PORTRAIT OF ADAM AND EVE

Some of the most overlooked and unread verses in Scripture are ones that sound a little something like this ...

"And _____ was the son of _____ from _____ ..."

When we come across these types of verses, called genealogies, the majority of us internally say, *Thank you, next,* and move on to the "good" stuff. If we're honest, it's easy to see these types of verses as interruptions. But what if some of the best insight is actually hidden and embedded in those few verses?

You see, the genealogy of Jesus in Luke 3:23-38 is one of those examples. In verse 38, we find Luke ending the genealogy of Jesus with, *"... the son of Adam, the son of God"* (Luke 3:38). Luke starts with Jesus, the Son of God, (Luke 1:35) and ends with Adam, the son of God. Why would Luke do this? To draw a connection for us between Jesus and Adam.

To begin to see Jesus in the Old Testament, the first place to look is Adam.

As we take a look at Adam, pay careful attention to the details revealed about him. First, Adam and his wife, Eve, were created in the likeness and image of God and put in a beautiful place called the Garden of Eden. Take out your Bible and take note of these highlighted key moments of Adam and Eve's lives that we will unpack in just a few minutes:

Adam and Eve were given *"dominion"* over creation
(Genesis 1:26).

Adam and Eve were told to *"Be fruitful and multiply and fill the earth"*
(Genesis 1:28b).

Adam and Eve were told to *"subdue"* the land
(Genesis 1:28b).

Adam and Eve were told to *"keep"* the land
(Genesis 2:15).

Adam and Eve were told not to eat the fruit.
(Genesis 2:17)

Adam and Eve were tempted by the serpent; they ate the fruit, and
sin entered the world. (Genesis 3:1-13)

— A NOTE FROM JOEL

The dignity of being made in the likeness and image of God should inform and direct our desires, ambitions and futures. Even more comforting: You and I did nothing to earn this dignity; it was a gift freely given to us by God Himself. Adam and Eve were given dignity before God ever told them to do anything.

All of the details surrounding these roles and responsibilities of Adam and Eve tell us God created humanity with dignity (being made in the image of God). That dignity came with a destiny (multiply, be fruitful, subdue, have dominion, keep/guard). This may be one of the most important things for us to remember not just as we look at the lives of Adam and Eve but also as we wake up each morning and step into our day ... Our dignity precedes our destiny.

01 | How does knowing you're made in the likeness and image of God reassure you in a situation you're facing right now?

To be made in the likeness and image of God also had royal connotations. The language of the Ancient Near East would describe Adam and Eve as viceregents, meaning they were living as actual representatives of God Himself on earth. To be a *vicegerent* is to reflect God's Kingship on earth.[2] This means Adam and Eve, and therefore all of humanity, were freely given the gift of dignity, wrapped up in royal privilege that came with royal expectations.

Lysa here. Sometimes I get confused when I see different names for the same or similar locations for events in the Bible. And I love learning clarifications that help me not get tripped up or confused. Here's something I just recently discovered: Whenever you read the term "Ancient Near East" it refers to the geographical location that encompassed Israel and the surrounding nations where the Israelites lived. This would include Mesopotamia, ancient Egypt, Persia, Syria, Israel, Jordan and Asia Minor. By the time we get into the New Testament this same general area is referred to as the "Greco-Roman World." It's a similar geographical area that was influenced and shaped by Greek and Roman culture that became prominent around the time of Jesus. So what does all of this mean to us? Anytime you read "Ancient Near East" the context is the Old Testament. Anytime you read "Greco-Roman World" the context is the New Testament.

02 | Read 1 Peter 2:9. What connection do you see between Adam and Eve having a royal identity and God calling us as believers *"a royal priesthood"*?

The expectations for Adam and Eve are seen clearly in Genesis 2:15 where God takes man and woman and places them in the Garden of Eden to *"work it and **keep** it."* The English word "keep" is a translation of the Hebrew word *"samar,"* which can be, and often is, translated as "guard or protect."[3] The implication of this word used for Adam and Eve in Eden meant that they were not just to be gardeners working the fields. No, they were also priests who had guarding and protecting duties. Sadly, this is also what is unfulfilled in their actions. Adam and Eve fail to *"samar,"* or guard and protect, Eden from the serpent, and they themselves are led into deception.

— A NOTE FROM JOEL

In 1 Chronicles 9:23, Israel's priests were told to *"samar"* the temple. In Nehemiah 11:19, the gatekeepers were "guardians/protectors."

03 Turn to Genesis 3 and record some highlights of Adam and Eve's conversation and overall interaction with the serpent.

A consistent theme we will turn to in this study is that Jesus is better. Jesus is the better Adam and Eve because Jesus faces the situations of temptation, but He is found as the faithful Son of God. Sadly, Adam and Eve are found falling short in their faith. Jesus will never fall short. Jesus will never get distracted by sin. He will never betray or abandon you. He will never stop guarding and protecting you.

04 How does this truth about Jesus' faithfulness encourage you in what you're walking through right now?

Let's return to that list of key moments in the lives of Adam and Eve and unpack some of them further as we begin to see their lives in connection with Jesus:

1. Adam and Eve were given dominion over creation, but Jesus is the creator and sustainer of all things.

John 1 tells us that all things were made through Christ and for Christ, and it is through Christ that all things are sustained (see Colossians 1:15-17). This should give us such immense confidence. Jesus not only cares for creation but is very present in creation: He was there in Genesis 1, and He is here now.

You may hesitate when reading that last sentence because there are things you're facing in your life right now where it doesn't seem Jesus is at work. There is chaos and confusion. Hurt and heartbreak. Divorce and disease. These are awful circumstances, but they are not evidence that Jesus doesn't care. These are all realities in a world where sin exists. Jesus is not a distracted king letting the world fall apart while He stands as an inactive bystander. He is the solution to the sin that's destroying people. Jesus wants us to see Him as the solution and to experience His presence and His kindness even in the middle of all that we're experiencing right now. He may not have caused it, but He will be so very present with us in it.

2. Adam and Eve were told to "be fruitful and multiply and fill the earth" (Genesis 1:28b).

Has this instruction ever felt confusing to you and seemed like it only applied to having children and filling the earth with more people? While the instruction to be fruitful does instruct us to multiply the population, the instruction to *"fill the earth"* is speaking to another assignment as well. This assignment from God is for image bearers (people made in the image of God) to fill the earth with evidence of God's goodness and God's faithfulness.

Sin disrupted perfection, but sin did not destroy this God-given assignment. We even see another connection here to the same instruction Jesus gives us in the New Testament, found in Matthew 28:19. Some of Jesus' last words were instructions to go and *"make disciples of all nations."* Isn't this fascinating? Adam and Eve received the same command as the disciples received from Jesus ... and those same instructions still apply to us today. Making these connections between the Old and New Testaments helps us to remember that the Bible is one continuous message. And Jesus is continuously present throughout all of Scripture.

He's in the Old Testament.
He's in the New Testament.

05 | How can you share the goodness and faithfulness of God with someone today? What does it mean to "make disciples of all nations"?

3. Adam and Eve were tempted by the serpent and ate the fruit, which ushered in sin. But Jesus conquered the power of the serpent and provided freedom from sin.

If there is one thing the enemy capitalizes upon, it's tempting us when we least expect it. It's something he's been working on since Genesis 3. It's interesting to consider the very real humanity of Adam and Eve. They are in the middle of this beautiful garden with all their needs and wants met. Everything is perfect. And instead of protecting Eden like God instructed them to do, they drop their guard.

When everything is calm and in place, we might forget to stay intentional. We may get lax in reading our Bible. We may get more inconsistent with praying. If we let our guard down, the enemy often starts his full-on assault of temptation.

The serpent successfully tempts Adam and Eve, which leads to a rupture in relationship with God, creation and God's people.

In the Gospels, we find Jesus in a similar predicament where He is tempted by Satan. But just before Jesus is tempted, we find Him in what may have been the most epic moment of His earthly life and ministry. (Matthew 3:13-17; Mark 1:9-11; Luke 3:21-22) After Jesus is baptized by John the Baptist, God the Father says to Jesus, *"You are my beloved Son; with you I am well pleased"* (Luke 3:22). Let's not skip this moment or overlook its significance. Right before Jesus is led in the wilderness to be tempted by Satan (the same serpent in Genesis 3), God the Father publicly affirms and confirms Him.

Not many would go to the wilderness willingly. The wilderness, for the Israelites, and even for us today, represents isolation and hardship. For Jesus, going into the wilderness of a physical desert meant treacherous dangers like wild animals and no guarantees of water supply. Yet Jesus was led into the wilderness where He would prove Himself to be the better and greater Adam.

Jesus was tempted but He was not deceived. Jesus used the words of Truth and showed us how powerful Truth is against the enemy's schemes. Adam and Eve knew God's words but lacked the trust to follow God's instructions when their own desires seemed more appealing.

To close today, we want to tell you something we say around Proverbs 31 Ministries often:

"Know the Truth. Live the Truth. It changes everything."

Oh, how this is so evident in the life of Jesus. He knew the Truth because He Himself is the Truth. (John 1:17) He lived out this Truth in everything He did and through everything He faced. And because of Jesus, everything changed. The ruptured relationship between God and His people, caused by sin, is repaired in Christ. He isn't just the better and greater Adam; He is the Savior King.

THE PORTRAIT OF MOSES

Lysa here. When you think about the Old Testament and the "founding fathers" of our faith, who comes to mind for you? I still remember being a little girl watching Charlton Heston, dressed in a red robe, with wild gray hair, hold up his arms and part the Red Sea. I was even more mesmerized when I found out this account of Moses was a true story.

I think many of us would say that Moses is one of the most important biblical figures in the Old Testament (possibly tied with David, whom we will also look at this week).

Historically, Moses is believed to be the author of the first five books of the Old Testament. He's a unique prophet of God who actually meets with the Lord face to face. When reading about the life of Moses, we find important similarities in the life of Jesus as well. Let's take a look at some of those:

First, both the mother of Jesus and the mother of Moses acted in courageous and selfless ways to ensure the safety and security of their sons. Jesus and Moses had such unusual beginnings to their lives.

01 | Read Exodus 1-2. What stands out to you about the birth and early life of Moses?

02 | Read Matthew 1:18-2:15. What similarities do you see in the birth of Jesus after reading about the birth of Moses?

Second, Moses and Jesus both had assignments to lead people out of enslavement. Moses led the Israelites out of the bondage of Pharaoh and Egypt. But Jesus would eventually lead all of those who place their faith in Him out of a bondage worse than that of Pharaoh — the grip of sin and death.

What Moses begins for the people of God, Jesus fulfills forever for the family of God.

But let's circle back to the beginning of this specific assignment God had for Moses. At the end of Exodus 3 and the beginning of Exodus 4, God calls Moses to represent Him to Pharaoh in order to release and free the Israelites. But it wasn't just Pharaoh who Moses had to convince. His first step was to convince the Israelites that it was time to leave their bondage and captivity.

Moses responds by saying, *"But behold, they will not believe me or listen to my voice ..."* (Exodus 4:1).

It's important to note that earlier, in Exodus 2:15, Moses had already tried to help the Israelites, but they essentially turned on him. So what's the key difference between Exodus 2 and Exodus 4?

In Exodus 2, Moses was trying to achieve something for his people out of his own might and work. However, now in Exodus 4, Moses was no longer working in his own strength and wisdom. He was being appointed and led by God.

When we look deeper into Exodus 4:1-17, we find Moses so focused on his weaknesses that he forgets God's power.

03 | Look at the words of Moses in Exodus 4:1, 4:10 and 4:13. Why do you think Moses responded in this way?

Where Moses says *"but ... they will ..."* (v. 1) and *"I am not ..."* (v. 10), God responds with *"I will be"* (vv. 12, 15). Moses disqualified himself, but God reminded Moses not of what disqualified him but of who was mighty with him: God Himself. God was the one who equipped Moses with the signs necessary to gain the trust of the Israelites. Though Moses angered God by asking Him to send someone else, God also provided Aaron to comfort and ease the anxiety of Moses.

— A NOTE FROM LYSA

God providing Aaron for Moses gives me a greater awareness to be even more thankful for the people I do everyday life alongside. I know I couldn't do ministry without the Aarons who fill in the gaps where I feel incapable or unable. Recognizing that God places people in community to help one another fulfill the assignments He has for them gives such an added layer of purpose to relationships. We share sorrows and celebrations, yes. But I want to always remember we share greater assignments from God as well.

In spite of the fact that God called Moses, Moses let his doubts and insecurities feed a distrust of God. And so often the same is true for us. Whether our trust issues are rooted in internal insecurities and insufficiencies or external obstacles that make us afraid, God reveals Himself as *"I will be."* This is our promise to hang on to in the middle of our own trust issues.

God never told Moses to bring the power. Moses was simply told to bring the words. You see, Moses' job was to be obedient to God. God's job was everything else. And as Moses navigated through this conversation with God, he learned how to practice obedience.

God wasn't asking Moses to play every part. Moses was only supposed to play his part. God would bring the power. God would bring the strategy. God would bring all the plans together. And God would certainly bring the victory. And the same is true for you and me.

04 | What assignment has God put before you today that you're struggling to trust Him fully in?

Feel encouraged that your job is simply to be obedient to God. He will lead you with what to say, what to do and how to move forward. Moses struggled with the reality of his insecurities, but his desire was to be obedient to God, even though his obedience was imperfect at times. This gives us a portrait of the Messiah, and one of the best ways to see all of this clearly is in the life of Jesus.

Jesus models the better way for us to handle our trust issues when we are faced with an assignment we wouldn't choose or even suffering in circumstances we didn't cause. We see this so beautifully lived out in Matthew 26:36-39 in the Garden of Gethsemane. Jesus displayed the perfect example of crying out to God in complete distress in His humanity, but He immediately backed it up with *"... nevertheless, not as I will, but as you will"* (Matthew 26:39).

The author of Hebrews even says that Jesus *"learned obedience through what he suffered"* (Hebrews 5:8).

05 | What surprises you about this verse? What encourages you about this verse?

You see, we can have questions and doubts in the midst of what God is asking us to do or even in the suffering we feel, but just like Moses and Jesus model for us, let's never forget the God who is "I Am" even in these places. We have no idea what could be on the other side of obedience!

The obedience of Moses created greater trust in God, and the outcome was the liberation of God's people. This paints a beautiful portrait of expectation for the greater Moses: Jesus. Jesus' life of obedience ultimately led Him to the cross for the liberation of humanity from sin and death. What a gift God gave us in knowing the story of Moses so we could see in an earthly sense what Jesus accomplished in an eternal sense.

He was "I Am" for Moses, and He was "I Am" through Jesus. And He will be "I Am" in whatever you're facing right now, too, friend.

DAY THREE

THE PORTRAIT OF JOSHUA

Lysa here. Yesterday we talked a lot about trust and obedience. I've found in my own life that the more I trust God, the more I choose to do things His way. But isn't it also true that the more we do things His way, the more we learn to trust Him? Trust and obedience go hand in hand. This wasn't just a key lesson for Moses to learn, but it's a continual theme and necessary practice we see in God's people throughout the entire Old Testament.

God promises His people to care for them, but they must obey Him and trust Him.

One of the most important aspects of God's relationship with Israel is the promise of rest in the promised land. Tragically, because of Moses' disobedience, which put on display a lack of trust in God, Moses would not enter the promised land. Instead, his assistant and disciple, Joshua, would take up the reins of leadership and lead Israel into the promised land.

Now, let's lean in here ... because there are so many interesting similarities between Joshua and Jesus you may have never considered.

The similarities between Joshua and Jesus start first with their names. In English, their names are different. But in Greek, "Jesus" and "Joshua" are actually the same name. One scholar has said, "Jesus was named after Joshua."[4] This becomes important in the book of Hebrews as the connection between Joshua and Jesus is established.

But let's take a closer look at who Joshua is and his responsibility in the Old Testament.

In Numbers 27:17, Moses looks forward to the future care of the Israelites after his death and asks the Lord to appoint a shepherd in his place. Without Moses, what would the Israelites do? Moses worries, *"who shall go out before them and come in before them, who shall lead them out and bring them in, that the congregation of the LORD may not be as sheep that have no shepherd."*

The imagery here of a shepherd and his sheep is rich with meaning. Sheep without a shepherd go astray and find themselves in dangerous situations because the shepherd provides care, security, provision and ultimately direction for the sheep. God would not let the *"sheep"* go astray, so He appointed Joshua to be the next *"shepherd"* of Israel (Numbers 27:17).

— A NOTE FROM JOEL

Rest is an important theme in the Bible, and it speaks to both the absence of conflict and the presence of peace. To be at rest is to know all is well and as it should be. The only way we can find true rest is when we find our rest in Jesus. As the church father Augustine said once of God, "You have formed us for yourself, and our hearts are restless till they find rest in you."[5]

Joshua was appointed to be the "shepherd" that would lead the Israelites into the promised land, but John 10:10-11 tells us that, even more so, Jesus embodies this for us: *"The thief comes only to steal and kill and destroy. I came that they may have life and have it abundantly. I am the good shepherd. The good shepherd lays down his life for the sheep."*

One of the key responsibilities of the shepherd was to lead the sheep to green pastures so they could rest. Joshua, as the "shepherd" of the Israelites, was tasked with the important responsibility to lead them into the green pastures of the promised land they had desperately longed for.

01 | When you think about your current needs and circumstances, how might you begin to see more of Jesus as your Good Shepherd leading you to rest?

Joshua did lead the Israelites into the promised land where they thought supernatural rest would be theirs. But when they arrived in Canaan (their promised land), all was not as they hoped. We can all relate to the Israelites in getting caught off guard by problems that come with our version of "promised lands."

02 | Have you ever hoped for something, but when it finally arrived, it ended up being different than what you expected? How did this affect you?

The Israelites longed for permanent rest, but they only found temporary relief. Hebrews 4:8 gives us a really important insight into what happened with Joshua and the Israelites in these moments:

"For if Joshua had given them rest, God would not have spoken of another day later on."

The author of Hebrews reminds us that the rest the Israelites experienced in the promised land was temporary rest. How do we know this? Because a few hundred years later, King David spoke of a future rest for the people of God. (Psalm 95)

Joshua led the people faithfully into their earthly inheritance of Canaan, but they never ultimately experienced the rest they thought this promised land would give them. The unrest the people experienced, even in the promised land, was due to their disobedience to God. Though God warned them to stay faithful to His instructions so they would be blessed, they went against Him. They worshipped and followed after the false gods of the surrounding nations, bringing the consequences of disobedience upon themselves. (See Deuteronomy 11:26-29.) So, though God kept His promise and honored the people, the people didn't honor Him in return. This reminds us of Adam and Eve in the Garden of Eden. They had amazing provision given to them by God but still disobeyed Him. And sadly, we do this very same thing. We long for peace and rest but we often don't do what God says ... or we suffer because others around us don't do what God says. In both cases, the result is unrest.

This is where we see another connection between Joshua and Jesus. Both of them were faithful, but they were leading people who had a propensity toward disobedience. Though Joshua was obedient in his assignment to lead the people to a place where they could have had physical rest, the sins of the people robbed them of that. Joshua delivered them to the promised land but could not deliver them from sin. Ultimately, Jesus provides what Joshua could never give: forgiveness of our sins and rest for our souls *even in* hard circumstances and pain. Like we've said before about these portraits of Jesus, Joshua could only do in part what Jesus would later do in full.

So, like we discussed at the beginning of today, the way Joshua and Jesus led people who were prone to go astray resembles the relationship a shepherd has with his sheep. Joshua was a good shepherd, but Jesus is the Great Shepherd. (Hebrews 13:20)

Through His death, burial, resurrection and ascension into heaven, Jesus leads His people into eternal security and peace with Him.

But how is Jesus our Great Shepherd today if He's no longer physically present with us? The Holy Spirit, or the Spirit of Jesus, is inside of us as believers. When Jesus was here on earth, His physical presence with people was limited to whoever He was with at that moment. If He was with Peter walking the shores of Galilee then He wasn't physically present with people in the Garden of Gethsemane at the same time. But when Jesus ascended into heaven, He promised the gift of His Spirit that would be with all believers all the time.

— A NOTE FROM JOEL

The Holy Spirit is referred to in different ways throughout Scripture. The Spirit is called *"The Spirit of God"* (Ephesians 4:30), *"The Holy Spirit"* (Ephesians 1:13) and *"The Spirit of Christ"* (Romans 8:9). All three terms describe the same thing — God, the Holy Spirit.

03 Pause on this truth for just a minute. We have the very Spirit of Jesus, our Good Shepherd, who indwells and empowers us so we can live with confidence and courage and be comforted in our troubles. Not only is Jesus near, but He is present and within us through the Spirit. Read Philippians 1:19, Acts 16:7 and Galatians 4:6 and reflect upon their meaning. Write some of the truths contained within these Scripture verses that stand out to you.

The journey to the promised land was by no means an easy one. It was a long and difficult road paved with tragedy and turmoil. It was filled with overwhelming obstacles that seemed to shout, "Your God is not for you. Just look around you! This sure doesn't look like the road to fulfilled promises to me."

Maybe you're in a place like that right now. You're trying to cling to the promises of God and move forward in faith, but difficult circumstances seem to be shouting so loudly in opposition. It feels as if your difficult situation is daring you to doubt the goodness of God ... inviting you to label Him forgetful or even unfair ... tempting you to panic and give up hope.

We've all been there. We've all walked through seasons where our circumstances don't seem to line up with God's promises. But just because they don't line up doesn't mean God isn't going to show up.

Because of Jesus, we don't have to go somewhere else for peace and rest. He is the Good Shepherd to us because He helps us find green pastures. Indeed, He is our peace. He is our rest. Peace and rest for our souls isn't a physical journey we must take one day into the promised land but rather a spiritual practice of trust we get to participate in today.

04 | Read Matthew 11:28-30. How do these words comfort you right now in what you're facing?

Oh, friend, our God is a God of completion. He makes promises, and then He fulfills them. (Hebrews 10:23) Yes, the journey may be harder than we expected. The road to our promise may not look anything like we thought it would. But we can rest assured there is never a question of whether or not our God will be faithful.

Jesus is evidence of His faithfulness to us! We can trust Him. Even when life takes unexpected twists and turns. Our God is a promise-keeping God.

THE PORTRAIT OF DAVID

Lysa here. Have you ever wanted something so badly that you'd do almost anything to get it? Maybe you even overlooked some big red flags, pushed through resistance and carried on with your own plan. I know I have. I've thought that my way was the best way without really considering God's way.

01 | How do you personally relate to wanting solutions to circumstances more than trusting God's instructions and heeding His warnings?

The Israelites certainly walked this path when they demanded a human king, against the Lord's instruction. We're going to spend an entire day in Week 4 talking about kings, but for the purposes of today's study, let's locate where the Israelites are in their journey and history, which will lead us to David.

After being freed from Egypt, wandering in the wilderness, and coming against numerous tests and trials, the Israelites, led by Joshua, eventually entered the promised land. You're already an expert on this because of what we studied yesterday! After this came a period when judges served as leaders of the Israelites, but what the people longed for was a true king to lead them.

— A NOTE FROM JOEL

"Yahweh" is the intimate name of God for the Israelites; it was a name that reminded the people of the greatness of God and that they were His possession and inheritance. (Deuteronomy 4:19-20; 32:8-9)[6]

Where did they get this idea? They observed the ways of the pagan nations around them who all had physical, human rulers sitting on a throne, and Israel longed for something that was never intended for them. We know they already had a king — Yahweh — but the Israelites continued to look for ways to have their needs met outside of God. Another example of this is their longing for rest that we studied yesterday. It wasn't that their longing for rest was wrong; it was that they often sought ways to achieve what they wanted through rebellion and self-reliance.

Longings are complicated feelings. They are desires with an intensity and drive behind them that make it seem like we must have what we want right now. When our motives are pure and our hearts are in a good place, we are more likely to trust God even when we don't understand His timing. But, when we are disoriented or in an unhealthy place, our longings can become misdirected. We end up seeking things that have the false promise of fulfillment and satisfaction but only bring more confusion, deeper bondage and entrapment.[7]

For example, longing for connection in a relationship is a great thing. But if that relationship leads us to compromise and unhealthy patterns, the longing we felt won't truly be satisfied. And now, on top of the continued longing for a true relationship, we'll have layered on hurt and pain.

02 | Pause to consider something you are longing for right now. Think through the possible outcomes of inviting God into this longing. Then think through the possible outcomes of not inviting God into this longing. Write your thoughts here.

Back to the Israelites. Despite God's warnings that an earthly king wouldn't be best for them, they wanted what they wanted. Their first king, Saul, looked like a king and presented himself with the kind of pride and confidence you'd expect from such a leader. However, he stopped relying on God, and his concern was more to protect his position than to truly help the people. People didn't factor in that a human king is still so *very human.*

This is why Saul's kingship didn't last. God chose David to be the next leader of Israel. Not only was David appointed, but he actually became the "ideal king" that all other kings were compared to throughout the books of 1 and 2 Kings.[8] This "ideal" was defined by important aspects of leadership that God desired for kings of Israel, such as:

1. All human kings were to submit to the great King of heaven and earth.
2. The heart of the king mattered much more than what the king accomplished.
3. The kings were to lead the people to pursue holiness and live in such a way that it would be evident to the surrounding nations that the Israelites were the people of God.

David is unique and worth our attention compared to all the other kings of Israel because he exemplified these aspects of kingship. David knew who was the true King, and he made obeying God and honoring God's ways a high priority. We see this when David had an opportunity to slay the reigning king, Saul. David relented and said, *"The LORD forbid that I should do this thing to my lord, the LORD's anointed, to put out my hand against him, seeing he is the LORD's anointed"* (1 Samuel 24:6).

David could have even seen this moment as a "God moment" for him to claim his kingship, but David knew it was not the right time to act. Despite the fact that Saul sinned and even tried to murder David, David didn't take the opportunity for revenge because he knew Saul's life wasn't his to take.

David could have so easily justified taking action against Saul but he instead left Saul in God's hands and didn't retaliate. He yielded to God's will. This is one of the places where we can see David trusting God in such a similar way to Jesus. When Jesus' life was being threatened just before He went to the cross, He prayed, *"not what I will, but what you will"* in Mark 14:36c.

Learning to trade my will for God's will has made such a shift in my perspective and honestly brought so much peace to my mind. Instead of always trying to solve my problems myself and ask God to bless my suggestions, I've decided to pray out loud, "I'm trading my will for Thy will because I'm so confident You will, God."

03 | How can you trade a suggestion you've been making to God in this way today?

In David we find a king who understands he serves under the great King and does so faithfully because of the condition of his heart.

04 | Read 1 Samuel 16:7. What do you see further explained about the condition of our hearts? How does this speak to you?

05 | What else do we learn about the condition of David's heart in 1 Samuel 13:14 and Acts 13:22?

The heart posture of King David is in fact what gave his kingship value and worth. The title of king itself was meaningless without a heart attuned to God. However, even though David's heart was yielded to God, his life was still complicated. For all the good he did, he also caused some immense damage to himself, his family and even the kingdom of Israel because of his sins. And here's where we see that, as great of a king as David was, the one victory he could not win was the victory over sin. Only Jesus could fill the gap that sin created between God and man. Remember, we've examined before that these figures in the Bible were portraits of Jesus, but they were always imperfect. They could only do in part what Jesus could do in perfection.

Jesus' sinless life brought hope, peace and the gift of eternal life to so many others. David's sins, like our own sins, brought tragedy, hurt and heartbreak on himself and so many others. Here are some of those examples summarized below:

- David slept with Bathsheba, a woman who was not his wife. (2 Samuel 11:1-5)
- He covered up his transgression by orchestrating the murder of Uriah, Bathsheba's husband, when she informed David she was pregnant. (2 Samuel 11:6-27)
- David, trusting in his own might, sinned against God by taking a census of Israel. (1 Chronicles 21:1, 21:8)
- David broke the Law by having more than one wife as prescribed for the king. (Deuteronomy 17:17)

Sometimes it can be confusing how this same flawed king can also be referred to as a man after God's own heart. One of the reasons is because, when confronted with sin, he responds out of humility and not a defensive pride. He allows God to break him rather than let his pride overtake him. David repents out of a true brokenness of his heart. His response is short and uncomplicated. He doesn't blame. He doesn't justify. He doesn't make excuses. He doesn't minimize what he's done. He owns his sin. You can see his response in 2 Samuel 12:13.

David experienced deep pain as a result of his sin, but his story still serves as a source of encouragement and hope for us. It displays tragedy and brokenness but shows that God can still work for good in the midst of it all. And best of all, God didn't leave David on his own to figure it out.

06 | No matter our past, we can choose today to be a people after God's own heart — placing our faith in Jesus, humbly choosing to own our sin, repent and let God's grace and forgiveness flood in. Look at the phrases below, and write down which ones you need to tend to today and why.

- Owning my sin.

- Repenting out of true brokenness.

- Not blaming others or justifying what I've done.

- Not making excuses for sinful behaviors I know I need to stop.

- Not minimizing or covering up what I've done.

- Receiving God's grace and forgiveness.

- Giving God's grace and forgiveness to another.

When thinking about King David and King Jesus, there's one last story to highlight. One of the most sobering moments in David's life takes place as his son Absalom initiates a revolt and forces David into exile. (2 Samuel 15) It is a tragic moment not only for David but for all of Israel.

And in 2 Samuel 15:23-30, we are told that all the people of the land wept, and David wept, too, as he ascended the Mount of Olives. The path David took to escape here was a known escape route from Jerusalem.

In this instance, David leaves his city and his people and goes up the mountain in defeat. The tears that David sheds are forced upon him because of the rebellion, revolt and insurrection led by his son Absalom.

Jesus had a similar experience at the same mountain, but the circumstances were much different. When we read Luke 19:28-41, we find Jesus coming down from the Mount of Olives, welcomed by all the people. Matthew's account of this event says they were proclaiming, *"Hosanna to the Son of David! Blessed is he who comes in the name of the Lord! Hosanna in the highest!"* (Matthew 21:9). The crowds were essentially welcoming Jesus as a conquering king and expecting Jesus to deliver them from Roman oppression and subjugation, rescuing them the same way King David did.

Joel here. The repetitive theme of exile and oppression follows the people of God into the New Testament. However, rather than the Philistines, Assyrians or Babylonians, the national power of the time was the Roman world. So the Israelites in the New Testament faced a similar hardship as their ancestors in the Old Testament.

07 The response of Jesus in the middle of this scene is almost shocking. We would expect Jesus to welcome the celebration, adoration and applause. However, read Luke 19:41 and record what it says Jesus does. Write your thoughts about this. Does Jesus' reaction surprise you?

David weeps as he leaves his city and his people behind because of defeat. Jesus weeps over His people, His city and all of humanity, at the bondage of sin and death they are in.

David leaves in defeat because he suffered a great loss. But the greater David, Jesus, enters the city and ultimately defeats the greatest enemy of all, sin and death, through His own death and claims victory forever.

We can all relate to David's weeping. Our lives are riddled with evidence we live in a broken world — loss, hurt, death, betrayal, heartbreak and relationship breakdowns. But might we also remember Jesus' weeping as well. He hurts when we hurt. And that's the exact reason He made a way for us to one day enter His eternal Kingdom, where there will be no more sorrow and no more weeping.

As we end today, write out a prayer thanking Jesus for being our ultimate King who holds the keys of victory over sin and death yesterday, today and forevermore.

THE PORTRAIT OF ESTHER

What if I told you that we can actually find Jesus in the book of Esther? You might not remember seeing Him in those pages before, but I can assure you ... He's there.

Yes, Esther may be an unexpected place to look for Jesus in the Old Testament. But I think you'll soon see that there is arguably no better book in the Bible than Esther for us to establish our own footing in the unexpected, unseen and sometimes completely upside-down nature of life.

Let's start with what makes Esther so unique. First, it is only one of two books named after a woman in the Bible, the other being the book of Ruth. Second, the name of God is not found in the text of the book, and Esther omits important biblical themes that are throughout the Old Testament (examples include: Sinai covenant, Israelite traditions, Jerusalem, the temple and the land of Israel). In other words, Esther is absent of what's standard in the other books of the Old Testament. But let's take a moment and consider what is present in Esther. We find heartbreaking circumstances, complicated relationship dynamics, unexpected betrayal and people who are just flat-out mean.

These details make the story of Esther relevant to what many of us find ourselves feeling today. In the midst of our own unexpected hardships, it can feel like our lives are anything but normal. And when things feel "off" and different than what we've been hoping and praying for, it can seem like Jesus is so very absent.

... We feel stuck and see little to no activity when it comes to God's movement in things we're begging Him to change.
... We feel awkward and anxious in the places we're supposed to experience Him, like church, small group or even time with Christian friends.
... We cry out to Him to give us something but feel like we're met with silence on the receiving end.

Sometimes it's hard for us to honestly admit we feel these realities, but voicing and admitting where we're struggling is a vital thing for us to do. And God is not afraid of your honest cries and guttural prayers. In fact, when we finally see Jesus in human form in the New Testament, even He cried out to God because He was feeling overwhelmed with sorrow to the point of death and asked God to change the plan set in motion. (Mark 14:32-42)

Even in His perfect divinity, Jesus experienced the feelings of humanity. He knew overwhelming sorrow and the brutality of being betrayed and abandoned. If we remember this when we read His teachings, we can know He taught from a place of understanding the challenges of being human. And in His mercy, He is showing us how to better navigate the pitfalls of heartbreak so we don't get off track in the midst of confusing and threatening circumstances.

01 | How does this bring you comfort in what you're facing today?

We will examine the portrait of Jesus we can see through the life of Esther in just a minute. After all, Esther certainly knew about confusing and threatening circumstances. But first, let's look for the presence of God through all the unlikely happenings in her story. Here are some key moments to examine:

- Esther was an orphan of Jewish descent who was taken care of by her uncle Mordecai and chosen for the royal court. (Esther 2) This would have been incredibly unlikely because she was both an orphan and a Jew, but *somehow* Esther was picked and given special consideration from Hegai, who was in charge of the women.

- *At just the right time,* Mordecai discovered a plot to overthrow the king and told Esther. (Esther 2:19-23)

- Haman, a Persian court official who winds up being the villain of this story, saw Mordecai not bowing to him (because bowing would have been idolatry). Haman had murder in his heart, not just for Mordecai but for all of Mordecai's people, the Jews. (Esther 3:4-6) At first it seems like this turn of events works in favor of evil, *but not for long.*

- Mordecai asked Esther to speak on behalf of her people. Esther, the orphan girl, who not only made the ***unlikely journey*** into the royal court but was established as the queen, had direct access to the king at this pivotal time. (Esther 4)

- ***The king couldn't sleep one night*** and had an assistant read all the accounts of people who had done "memorable deeds." ***Of all the accounts,*** the king heard Mordecai's story and desired to make sure Mordecai was honored. (Esther 6)

- When the king considered how to honor Mordecai, Haman, the enemy of Mordecai, was asked to give his opinion on how to honor this friend of the king. ***In irony,*** Haman told the king how to honor Mordecai and then had to lead Mordecai around in a procession in his honor. (Esther 6)

- In a last-ditch effort, Haman built a gallows for Mordecai. But after Esther exposed Haman's evil plot, ***Haman was hanged on his own gallows.*** (Esther 5:9-14; 7:5-10)

Look at all of the statements above that are italicized. There are so many more examples, but these moments reveal the presence and provision of God. Sometimes, as things get harder we can see evidence of God even more clearly. In the story of Esther, the twists and turns are not coincidental. The same is true in our lives. God's presence may be unseen, but He is still working.

02 | Where are you being challenged to have faith in God's "unseen" activity right now?

So what about seeing Jesus through this story? Now that we've seen the presence of God more clearly, let's look at the vision or portrait of Jesus through Esther and her life. There are so many startling similarities to the life of Jesus.

Let's first look at the timing of both the life of Esther and the life of Jesus (in the flesh). In both situations the people felt that God had stopped speaking to them and acting on their behalf. They were living in what felt like the silence of God. Esther disrupted that period of silence. But Jesus ended it completely. For the Israelites who were living in the reality of exile in the time of Esther, and for the Israelites who were experiencing a different kind of exile under the Romans in the time of Jesus, the silence was deafening. But silence is not proof of the absence of God; it's proof that God is working in ways we can't see or hear.

03 | How does this truth encourage you personally today?

Have you ever wondered what happened after the end of the Old Testament and before the New Testament began? When Matthew 1 begins, the people of God have experienced an immense silence from God. In fact, the period of time between the end of Malachi (the last book of the Old Testament) and the beginning of Matthew 1 (the first book of the New Testament) is often referred to as "400 years of silence." The birth of Jesus ended that silence.

Just like Esther, Jesus entered human history in a time of great need. But, like we've seen with the other "portraits" this week, what Esther does for a time in history, Jesus does for all of history. Esther was sent to save the Jewish people of her time. Jesus was sent to save all of humanity for eternity. Again, through this story of Esther, we get to see a human situation play out that shows us a glimpse in the physical realm of what Jesus is doing in the spiritual realm.

In the story of Esther, Haman (the villain) believed he had created a foolproof plot to murder and completely annihilate the people of God. If Haman's plan had worked, Esther herself would have been killed. In the life of Jesus, the enemies of Jesus (King Herod, the Pharisees and Sadducees, and Pontius Pilate) believed they had created a foolproof plan to get rid of the Messiah and to overthrow His reign. Ultimately, the real villains weren't the men who came against Jesus. The villain was the enemy, the evil one: Satan.

But the irony is that the very plan of Satan is used in the redemptive story of Jesus. The enemy sets Jesus on the journey to the cross, but with every step Jesus takes, the enemy is closer to defeat. In a similar reversal, the very agenda, plan and strategy of Haman was used against him to bring about his own demise.

In both stories we find similarities:

- There was an evil plan.
- There was an enemy.
- Innocent people were going to be destroyed if someone didn't step in to save them.
- A hero came from humble beginnings and looked nothing like what the people expected.
- The hero remained humble and honored God in their approach to handling the dire situation.
- The hero was uniquely positioned by God to fulfill the plan of God.
- The hero set aside what was best for them for a greater good purpose.

To close today's teaching and this week of portraits, let's look at the correlation between Esther and Jesus through the lenses of "shadow" and "sun."[9] Like we talked about in the introduction to this week, every shadow reminds us that something brighter and bigger exists. So the shadow points us to a larger truth. Go back and read the introduction to this week for a refresh if you need to.

SHADOW:
Esther initiates a three-day fast that begins on Passover. (Esther 4:16) ●

SUN:
○ Jesus' journey to the cross begins after He finishes the Passover meal (John 18:28) and leads to the three-day period of his death and resurrection.

SHADOW:
After Esther's fast, she clothes herself in royalty. (Esther 5:1) ●

SUN:
○ After Jesus' death and burial, He is resurrected *"in glory"* (1 Corinthians 15:43). The idea of glory connects to the concept of being *"clothed"* with glory (Job 40:10).

SHADOW:
Esther presents herself before the king, who accepts her. (Esther 5:2) ●

SUN:
○ Jesus presents Himself to the Father, and the Father says He is pleased with Jesus. (Matthew 3:17)

SHADOW:
As an outcome of Esther's bravery to approach the king, Jews are saved, and even gentiles take part in the community of God's people. (Esther 8:17) ●

SUN:
○ The outcome of Jesus being accepted by the Father is the salvation of Israel (Matthew 15:24) and gentile inclusion. (Colossians 2:11; Acts 11:18; Galatians 3:8)

Now, let's pray together as we conclude Week 1. *Father God, I praise You today for how far You have carried me in everything I've walked through. I'm so grateful today for the gift of Your Son, Jesus. Thank You for the ways You are opening my eyes and allowing me to see Jesus in a whole new light in the Old Testament. I pray for a discerning mind and tender heart as I lean in to what You may have for me. God, I trust You. I know that You were never absent for a single moment in Scripture, and You're never absent in my story, either. I praise You today for the fact that, no matter what I face, I will never be alone. In Jesus' Name, Amen.*

WEEK
two

2

THROUGH PROPHECIES

INTRODUCTION *to prophecies*

Joel here! This week we're going to look at seeing Jesus in the Old Testament through prophecy. Lysa will define that term for you in more detail in just a minute. But basically prophecy was used by God so the people could see something either in the present or in the future. It reminds me of bifocal glasses, which provide comfort in being able to see things close and far away.

I've had glasses since I was 9 years old. Back then, I had the Harry Potter gold-rimmed glasses that were definitely not cool. Somehow those spectacles have made a big comeback today. Who would've thought?! Needless to say, I have a strong prescription. When I say "strong," I mean sometimes I feel like I can get a glimpse into the immediate future if I look through my glasses hard enough!

Not too long ago, I went to the eye doctor to get my eyes checked. Glasses and contacts are expensive, so I asked my eye doctor about LASIK eye correction surgery. My doctor looked at me with a sideways grin and began to say "Well ..." followed by a long, drawn-out pause. He continued to tell me that, as I got older, my eyes, regardless of surgery, were going to need glasses. He then told me about these amazing glasses that I would eventually need ... you know, the kind that have two levels: the lower level for reading and close-up vision, and the upper level for seeing far away.

Bifocals at my age? No way. I mean, Lysa has bifocals, but she's celebrated a few more birthdays than me!

A note from Lysa: No, Joel, I use readers. And just so you remember, with age comes wisdom, which basically means, if we disagree on something, chances are I'll be right. Thank you very much and have a nice day.

Lysa, you got me there. Proverbs 16:31 does remind us that *"gray hair is a crown of glory."* Haha. Anyhow, all this talk about bifocals got me thinking that they are a perfect image to help us understand biblical prophecy.

Throughout the Old Testament, prophecies sometimes had a multi-layered application. Sometimes a prophecy had a more *immediate fulfillment* that would boost people's confidence in God. Other times, the prophets spoke of prophecies that wouldn't be fulfilled for hundreds of years, if not longer. Then, there were also *bifocal* types of prophecies where a portion would be fulfilled sooner, and an additional part would be fulfilled later.

When it comes to the prophecies specifically telling of the coming Messiah (also known as messianic prophecies), we find both the distant-future type of prophecies and the bifocal types of prophecies. In fact, just like we learned last week about the various portraits that were *shadows* of the coming Christ, these prophecies work in a similar way. Prophecies are like a shadow pointing to a future and final fulfillment of *when* Jesus would eventually come and *what* He would eventually fulfill.

Lysa here. Do you ever get confused by the term "prophecy?" Me too. So let's clearly define what this word means and how this word and its other forms are used in the Bible. Here's an overview of how we'll define the word and the different forms it will take in our study, as well as in Scripture as a whole:

Prophecy (noun): A message concerning future events and how they relate to people.

Prophesy (verb): The act or occurrence of prophecy being shared or announced.

Messianic Prophecy: A future promise that is specific to the promised Messiah (who we know is Jesus) coming in the flesh as the King who will bring justice and ultimately right all of the wrongs that result from sin.

Prophet: The vessel to whom God would speak directly and who would convey the prophecies to other people.

Major Prophets: These books of the Old Testament: Isaiah, Jeremiah, Lamentations, Ezekiel and Daniel. As a general rule, they are identified using the term *major* because of their length and focus on broader themes and topics. For example, one of the broader themes in the Major Prophets is holiness.

Minor Prophets: Also referred to as *The 12*. They include Hosea, Joel, Amos, Obadiah, Jonah, Micah, Nahum, Habakkuk, Zephaniah, Haggai, Zechariah and Malachi. These books are given the term *minor* because they are shorter and their messages are more narrowly focused. For example, there is a focus in Joel on the coming of the Holy Spirit.

Now that we're on the same page as far as terms, let's look deeper into what this means for our focus this week.

Even though prophecy probably isn't part of our daily vocabulary, it was actually quite familiar to the Israelites in the Old Testament. The pagan nations surrounding Israel used magic and divination as a means of conjuring up "prophecy" or seeing into the future. The Israelites were forbidden to practice this kind of magic. But they had prophets. And it wasn't unusual for them to receive, through a prophet, a message from God about the future. And although God had already spoken to the Israelites through the Law (God's commands for His people to live by), He also spoke through prophecy when there was a timely message related to a specific event for the people of Israel. The origin and source of the message was God, but He used prophets to communicate to His people.

The prophets played a major role in the history of God's people. Some of the prophets saw a once-mighty kingdom divide into two kingdoms, then finally collapse and be overtaken by foreign nations. This devastation was something they would have never expected, but it happened before their own eyes. Because they lived in times that were really, really hard, the people were desperate for messages from God.

Some of the prophets lived during a time period called the "Exile" when the Israelites were held in captivity by the Babylonians and Assyrians. This was a time of deep sorrow and pain when all hope seemed lost. The promises of God were still present but seemed so far away and definitely out of reach.

Finally, the "Postexilic" period was when the people of God were allowed to go back to their land and rebuild the temple, their walls, their city and homes. But what they rebuilt didn't compare to the previous temple and the glory of the city at the time of David and Solomon.

These historical moments are not just a back-then reality. They relate to our right-now experiences. Maybe you can understand the feeling of seeing something you've invested your heart and soul in shift from being strong and secure to being divided and in ruins.

Or maybe you feel like you're in the very center of the wilderness. It feels like exile ... Nothing is going right and it's been that way for a while. All of your hopes and dreams for the future feel out of reach.

... Maybe it's a family member struggling with addictions who refuses to get help.
... Or a friend who started dating someone you can't support, so your friendship has grown cold and distant.
... Or a financial setback that seems to worsen no matter how you try to turn it around.
... Or a business or ministry you had such high hopes for that isn't working out.
... Or a dream you've worked really hard to bring to life, but changing circumstances seem to be destroying it.

Maybe there are other situations where you can identify with the rebuilding process. You've gathered broken pieces of that part of your life and proclaimed that the Lord is Redeemer over it all. You've started looking for the good things God will surely work from all of this brokenness, but it's taking a lot of time.

... Maybe it's a relationship that fell apart, but you're fighting to put it back together.
... Or an adult child who walked away from the family but has started calling again.
... Or a job where you've had a boss that never saw your potential, but now there is a new leader for your department.

Friend, the prophecies that told of the coming Messiah took place in similar situations and circumstances. These prophecies reveal promises that still reign true today. And though we have the benefit now of living in the reality of a Messiah who has already come, we still long for the day He will return.

He was. He is. And He will forever be the Redeemer King.

And in that truth we have a bifocal promise of hope for today and hope for the future as we wait for complete redemption when Jesus returns. Old Testament scholar Christopher Wright says it this way: "The Old Testament tells the story that Jesus completes."[10]

This week, we will discover prophecies that tell of the coming of Christ and things He would accomplish. And we'll even touch on parts of books (circling back to the Major and Minor Prophets) that talk entirely about the coming Messiah. But no matter the focus of each day, we pray you experience a deeper personal connection with Jesus and continue to see evidence of God's intentional faithfulness in every aspect of Scripture. May these revelations bring you even greater confidence in how much you are thought of and cared for by God.

DAY SIX

PROPHECY FOUND IN THE PENTATEUCH

Remember what we learned last week about Adam and Eve? There are some details in their story we're going to take a deeper look at today. Surprisingly, the earliest prophecy of Jesus being born from a woman and of the future restoration He will bring is found in Genesis 3:15: *"I will put enmity between you and the woman, and between your offspring and her offspring; he shall bruise your head, and you shall bruise his heel."*

In the middle of God giving Adam and Eve the consequences caused by their sin and rebellion (also referred to as "the fall"), God promises that the woman and Satan will be enemies. God also brings judgment on the serpent, and it's in the punishment for his rebellious actions that we get a glimpse of what Jesus, the coming Messiah, will do to the evil one. The enemy will cause pain on all of the children that come from the woman but he will receive a much greater blow. Isn't it merciful of God to mention the future hope of what Jesus will do to the enemy in the midst of Adam and Eve being afraid of all that was unfolding?! Old Testament scholar Derek Kidner refers to this verse in Genesis 3:15 as "the first glimmer of the gospel."[11]

01 | What does this reveal to you personally about the mercy of God?

Genesis 3:15 is an example of the Law of First Mention. The Law of First Mention is where something is first seen or found (usually in the Old Testament) and then fulfilled, completed and/or furthered later in Scripture. Looking into the various mentions helps us more clearly define and understand biblical events and terms. So, here, the Good News is announced for the first time. And later, in the New Testament, it is fulfilled.

Lysa here. When Joel first taught our study team this principle, I was thinking this was a great thing for theologians to understand but not something a regular Bible study girl like me would ever use. And I couldn't have been more wrong. I now see such tremendous value in researching where a biblical principle or event is first seen or glimpsed in Scripture. Think of it this way: When you've been friends with someone for a long time, a pretty common question people might ask the two of you is, "Where did you meet each other?" That story becomes an important part of the larger story of your relationship. It gives the listener some context to your friendship. Setting the context for what we are reading in Scripture is important and helps us more clearly see the connections throughout the Bible's continuous story.

Now what does all of this have to do with prophecy? Because Genesis 3:15 shows us the hope for something to come, it is a very important prophecy. This single prophecy consists of three components:
1. The serpent named Satan.
2. The seed of the serpent.
3. The woman named Eve and her seed.

The Serpent/Satan
The serpent is unnamed in Genesis 3. However, we do know that the serpent was *"crafty"* (Genesis 3:1). He had an agenda that went beyond getting Adam and Eve to eat the forbidden fruit. He wanted to destroy humanity with sin and death. There is an intentionality behind the Hebrew word usage in Genesis 3:1 and 3:14 that is intended to lead the reader to see a connection between these verses. In Hebrew, the serpent goes from being a crafty (*arum*) serpent (Genesis 3:1) to becoming a cursed (*arur*) serpent (Genesis 3:14).[12] He intends to steal, kill and destroy, but in the end, his craftiness leads to the curse he will bear the consequences of most of all.

02 | Look up John 10:10 and write down what this verse reveals about the enemy and Jesus.

The Seed of the Serpent

The word *"offspring"* in Genesis 3:15 is the Hebrew word for "seed." This word is used twice to refer to both the seed of the woman and the seed of the serpent. But their "seeds" couldn't be more different.

The seed of the serpent are all those who follow the ways and works of Satan, the great, deceiving, ancient serpent (see Revelation 12:9). In the Gospel of John, the Pharisees are even referred to as children of the devil (John 8:44) even though they considered themselves children of Abraham. (John 8:39)

03 | Take a look at 1 John 3:7-10. What do these verses tell us are the distinguishing marks of being a child (seed) of God versus a child (seed) of Satan?

The Seed of the Woman

The "seed" of the woman in one sense represents all of humanity that will come from Eve for generations to come, including us today.

But in our research on this term we discovered that the seed of the woman referred to here is debated among Old Testament scholars. There is a dispute as to whether the "seed" should be understood as individual or collective.

The individual understanding of "seed" is the promised Messiah. It represents the individual person of Jesus because Jesus came from the lineage of Eve. However, some say that the "seed" is collective because all those who put their faith and trust in Jesus are also saved.

04 | Read Galatians 3:16. What word do you see pop up again?

What we see revealed in Galatians is not an "either/or" situation but a "both/and." The "seed" is individual, but the seed is also collective because in Jesus the Church is formed.

In Galatians 3:16, the Apostle Paul looks back on Genesis 3:15 and identifies the promised "seed" as Christ, furthering the promise made to Abraham. Abraham's offspring includes all people who put their faith in Jesus — also known as the Church! This represents the "Collective Descendants" as well. (See Romans 4:13; Romans 4:16-18; Galatians 3:8.)

And when God says *"he shall bruise your head, and you shall bruise his heel"* (Genesis 3:15), God prophesies that the offspring of the woman will *"bruise"* Satan's head, but Satan will *"bruise"* His heel. Though the enemy will try to derail God's mission to save the world through His Son, Jesus will claim ultimate victory over the serpent. And furthermore, that victory is a victory that the "Collective Descendants," or "Collective Seeds," of the Church share when we find ourselves in Christ.

1 John 5:4-5 says, *"For everyone who has been born of God overcomes the world. And this is the victory that has overcome the world—our faith. Who is it that overcomes the world except the one who believes that Jesus is the Son of God?"*

05 | How does knowing we share in the same victory as Christ encourage you? Where are you needing to see victory in your own life right now?

— A NOTE FROM JOEL

We will talk more about Abraham throughout our study, but it's important to remember that, in Genesis 12 (even though God chose Israel out of all the nations of the world), God promises that all the families of the earth will be blessed and brought together through Abraham and his family. The promise of Genesis 12 is the response and promise of unity that follows the tragedy of Genesis 11 and the tower of Babel when all the people are divided through diverse language. God wouldn't settle for division. He always desires union, and He promises to achieve this through Abraham and his family.

Like we have mentioned before, we have the benefit of being on the side of history that gets to read verses like Genesis 3:15 and immediately flip to passages in the New Testament where we can find Jesus. There, we can read about His life, death, burial, resurrection and ascension, and celebrate the fulfillment that was *only prophesied* at the time of Genesis 3:15.

Even though we get this advantage of reading the complete story of the Bible today, it's important to remember that the hundreds of pages separating Genesis 3 and the New Testament in our Bibles represent thousands of years that people waited for the promised Messiah.

In this truth, we find one of the requirements for biblical prophecy: dependence on God. God wants our complete dependence on Him and trust in His timing to bring about what He has promised and prophesied. When we patiently wait on God it develops in us the endurance we need for our faith to be strong.

Don't skip over a couple of key phrases from that last sentence too quickly: "patiently wait" and "endurance." That sounds a lot easier on paper than it actually is when we try to apply it to the difficult situations of real life.

"Oh yes, Lord? I have these prayer requests that I really want to talk to You about, but don't worry — I'm totally content with patiently waiting for these answers!"

I don't know if you're a much better Christian than me ... but my prayers don't always sound like that.

Most of us go through many seasons of waiting in our lives. But here's something you may have never considered before: It is this exact waiting assignment that connects our story with the story of the ancient people of God who waited so long for the coming Messiah. Make no mistake: Jesus was present but not walking among them in the flesh.

From Genesis through Malachi, the ancient people of God waited for the Messiah to come. Similarly, we await the return of Jesus to rescue us from the hurt of this broken world once and for all and to establish the new heavens and new earth. Before then, we have the everyday reality of waiting on Jesus to intervene in some way.

... Waiting for Jesus to reveal to us what our exact next step is in our career.

... Waiting to get married and start a family of our own.

... Waiting to get clear scans at that next doctor's appointment.

... Waiting for breakthroughs in complicated relationships that require so much emotional energy.

James 1:2-4 says, *"Count it all joy, my brothers, when you meet trials of various kinds, for you know that the testing of your faith produces steadfastness. And let steadfastness have its full effect, that you may be perfect and complete, lacking in nothing."*

06 | What part of these words challenges you the most? What part encourages you?

— A NOTE FROM LYSA

I will often pray this in the morning when I'm in a season of waiting: "God, I know You are good. You are good to me. You are good at being God. This situation doesn't feel good, look good or seem good in any way. But I can confidently declare that You are good in the midst of it all. I don't have to figure it all out. Help me know that and walk that out today. Guard my tired mind and my exhausted spirit from trying to do things that only You can do, Lord. My job is to be obedient to You. Your job is everything else. Amen."

When we find ourselves in a delay, we must determine to fill the gap between where we are now and what we are hoping to see happen by intentionally looking for Jesus' activity. And when we do this, we'll be able to better weather these waiting seasons, still believing Jesus is with us, and this reminds us that God is good.

That's probably not what you want to hear right now, friend. Waiting can feel excruciating. But just the fact that we woke up breathing this morning is evidence of His goodness. And even here ... He is close. We can take great comfort in knowing that, just because God is silent in one area of our lives, it doesn't mean He is silent in every area. And just because we can't see Jesus with our physical eyes, it doesn't mean He isn't here.

07 | Even if it's not the big answers to your prayers you've been waiting for, in what ways can you intentionally see God's activity in your life right now?

Isn't it amazing to dig into these prophecies and trace the faithfulness of God? What started as the very first glimmer of gospel hope has become complete in Christ. What was only promised in Genesis 3:15 was fulfilled on the cross where Jesus conquered sin, death and the enemy. And even in the middle of the tragedy of sin, God had Jesus in mind as the solution. Jesus has always been Plan A. And the next time the Messiah returns, He will do so not as a suffering servant but as the reigning, victorious King of heaven and earth.

But until then ... we get the privilege of leaning into Jesus as we endure, patiently wait and keep our faith in Him strong.

PROPHECY FOUND IN PRAYERS AND PRAISE

Lysa here. Have you ever prayed for something and waited for something, like we talked about yesterday, and then had to endure someone else getting the very thing you've been longing for? Me too. But it's made even more painful when the person gets what you've cried countless tears over and they put their blessing in your face in mean ways. I don't mean they unintentionally trigger pain with their answered prayer. I mean they are cruel to you in how they talk about what they got and you didn't. Maybe they judge you. Maybe they have an air of superiority when they talk to you. Or maybe they are just flat-out rude and criticize you as if all of what you are suffering could be different if you'd done what they did.

I had this happen when one of my most important relationships ended. Some people were kind with the heartbreak I'd experienced. A few others tried to shame me as if I hadn't given everything to try and save the relationship. They didn't know all the facts. They hadn't seen the brutality of what really happened. They didn't have an understanding that some relationships aren't just difficult — they are destructive to the one trying to save it.

If anyone knows the aches of not only patiently waiting but also enduring someone's cruelty in the midst of her heartbreak, it's a woman named Hannah from 1 Samuel. Hannah had a deep-rooted desire to be a mother but continued to wake up day after day with no children.

Her husband, Elkanah, had two wives, Hannah and Peninnah. Peninnah had multiple children with Elkanah, which made Hannah's longing even greater as she experienced the everyday presence of Peninnah's children, hearing them play, laugh and even be disciplined. Plus, Peninnah, noted in the Bible as Hannah's rival, was cruel to Hannah and provoked her to tears. Desperate situations create downcast emotions.

01 | Read 1 Samuel 1:10-11. What words are used to describe how much Hannah was feeling?

The term "rival" (צָרָה [ṣā·rā(h)]) is a Hebrew word depicting a competitive relationship that is unhealthy and is a result of one person being viewed as lower than the other. In this instance, because Elkanah loved Hannah more, it drove Peninnah into fury and she released that fury on Hannah.

But even when Hannah was being ridiculed by her *"rival,"* she did something that challenges and inspires me. She took her affliction and pain straight to the Lord. She went into the house of God in Shiloh and prayed.

02 | Read 1 Samuel 1:6. What word is used to describe Peninnah's relationship to Hannah?

Let's pause for a few minutes and camp out at Hannah's response. It's important to take note that Hannah not only went to the Lord, but she went to the Lord in *honesty*.

One of the most important things we can do in our desperation is go straight to the Lord. But it's almost equally important to go to the Lord in honesty. And this is not easy. Honesty has to be practiced — both with ourselves and God.

Hannah's pleading to God reveals how much she trusted Him. And she trusted God could handle her honesty as she cried out to Him, wishing her circumstances were different. We also notice that there isn't any evidence in the text that would lead us to believe God was going to respond with the miracle of giving her a child. That's what makes her so relatable to us today. She was an everyday, ordinary woman who was stuck in a desperate situation. And her desperation turned her to the Lord.

03 How does Hannah's example encourage you and challenge you?

Hannah's desperation reminds us to turn to God in uncertainty. And although she was never promised a child, she did plead for one.

Later in 1 Samuel 1, Hannah receives her answered prayer:

"And in due time Hannah conceived and bore a son, and she called his name Samuel, for she said, 'I have asked for him from the LORD'" (1 Samuel 1:20).

04 Pay close attention to those words *"in due time."* Write down why you think the Scriptures include this detail.

Now, before we finish reading Hannah's story, it's crucial we pause and address something here. There are many of you on the other side of these words who deeply relate to Hannah's anxiety, stress and sorrow. And reading verses like the one above causes your heart to sink. Because, although you can relate to her distress, you can't relate to her answered prayer. There isn't the miracle of a biological baby for every story.

But, friend, with great tenderness, I want to bear witness to your pain today and say that whatever you are believing God for, I am believing for it *with you*. God also hears you and sees you and is absolutely moved by your tears. Every single tear you've shed, in private or public, has not gone unnoticed by Him. The miracle He offers us sometimes does not change our circumstances or bring us the answers we so desperately want, but He does promise to remain near to us and to continue working in us.

And that is still a miracle. It just may not be the one you've been expecting. And no matter what you're facing, there is something God wants to teach you through Hannah's story today.

When we read 1 Samuel 2:1-10, we see Hannah's response of great praise. Here we find one of the most beautiful songs of worship and praise in the Old Testament. In fact, many Old Testament scholars are stunned by Hannah's words, articulation, imagery and the overall beauty of this song.

Hannah's response is framed in three important ways: her heart, horn and mouth. (1 Samuel 2:1) Now hang in here with us because this sequence is important ...

"... My heart exults in the LORD; ..."
(v. 1a, emphasis added)

For the ancient Israelites, the heart was the wellspring of emotion and volition. Meaning, the heart not only expressed feelings and desires, but the heart was also the seat of the will. Reclaiming this perspective is vital in how we understand ourselves and our actions. Our hearts pump out love, and where that love is aimed, actions will follow. In other words, what we love we look to. In Hannah's example here, all of the sorrow and despair she experienced in her life was channelled in her heart into a God-exulting prayer.

"... my horn is exalted in the LORD."
(v. 1a, emphasis added)

The horn being referred to here is a bull's horn, often used like a trumpet or like a megaphone, or even as a flask for oil. The thought of Hannah's *"horn"* being raised may feel odd to us in our current culture today. However, in the Ancient Near East, the metaphor of a wild bull was used to symbolize strength and victory.[13] When we look at drawings of people in the Ancient Near East, we find many pictures that tell mythological stories with people that have horns. Horns were seen as powerful. So what does the horn mean in the context of Hannah's prayer? Scholars often say that the horn imagery communicates God-given strength and dignity.[14]

"My mouth derides my enemies, because I rejoice in your salvation."

(v. 1b, emphasis added)

From our mouths come the opportunity and choice to bless or curse. Praise or plead. Ask questions or cast judgment. The mouth is an important part of the human body and also plays a vital role in how we relate to others. Hannah used her mouth to reflect what was true within her heart and in her raised horn, and she proclaimed the defeat of her enemies. It's interesting to see how different Bibles translate the Hebrew expression "mouth derides" (רָחַב, *rachav*), which can be literally translated as "mouth is wide."

05 | Using Biblegateway or Bible Hub, read 1 Samuel 2:1b and write down how these translations describe the action of *the mouth:*

ESV

NASB

NIV

NLT

CSB

Pro tip: Whenever you notice that there are different English words used in different translations of the Bible, this is a good indication that a Bible word study would be helpful. The difference in English words reflects that the translators were working hard to bring clarity to a word that may not be easily translated into English or that could be interpreted in different ways.

All of the translations share a common idea: The mouth speaks out against the enemy and proclaims victory because of the salvation that the Lord brings.

In order to further grasp what's happening here, we need to recall the usage of the *"horn"* just before this. As one Old Testament scholar said, "The image of a wide-open mouth (along with that of a raised horn) expresses the advantage of the speaker — who is free to say anything at all without hindrance — over the enemy."[15]

One final note here ... When Hannah says *"my enemies"* (1 Samuel 2:9), it would be easy to think this is in reference to Peninnah. After all, Peninnah was the one who was referenced earlier as Hannah's "rival" who absolutely mistreated her. But the Hebrew wording here is plural for "enemies," not singular for "enemy." This means Hannah does not make a personal attack against her own enemy but remembers that something bigger is going on beyond just her situation. So she speaks out against the enemies of God. Wow, what a perspective shift that Hannah gives us.

Hannah's trust and confidence in God becomes her advantage and actually enables her to speak directly from her heart, with strength and dignity, through her mouth.

When we think about a situation we may be facing right now, it's easy to isolate ourselves and attack people who are compounding hurt in our situation or seem to be the root of some of the problems we're having. But, friend, what would happen if we stepped back and remembered the ongoing, bigger conflict between God and His enemies? Whatever conflict we experience is set on the stage of a much bigger conflict.

06 | What does Ephesians 6:10-20 tell us about this bigger conflict happening?

So what about the prophecy in Hannah's story? This is where we will land today. The Lord, in His kindness, never leaves us to battle alone. In fact, the reason we can lift up our "horns" and proclaim out of our mouths with joyful hearts is because of God and the promise of the Messiah found a few verses later in Hannah's prayer. Look at 1 Samuel 2:10 to find the evidence of the prophecy we want to leave you with today:

*"The adversaries of the LORD shall be broken to pieces; against them he will thunder in heaven. The LORD will judge the ends of the earth; he will give strength to **his king** and **exalt the horn** of his **anointed**"* (emphasis added).

Who is the king? Well, the identity of the king can be found in the Hebrew word translated as *"anointed"* at the end of the sentence: מָשִׁיחַ *(mā·šîaḥ)*. This is the Messiah! Hannah is not speaking of some future, merely human king; she is prophesying of the *King of kings*, Jesus! In fact, this is the first time in the Old Testament that the Messiah is referred to as "anointed."[16]

What an incredible and important moment. Thousands of years before Jesus would be born in a little town called Bethlehem, Hannah's prophetic song had King Jesus in mind. Through such a long season of waiting, Hannah's pain actually led to the birth of her own son, but she also foretold God's one and only Son who would eventually come to earth. Through her waiting, she never gave up hope.

And though the people of God endured waiting as they longed for the Messiah, hope was already on the way.

We spent so much time learning about Hannah's story today because the humanity of the Bible matters and is sometimes so easily overlooked, especially in the complexities of the Old Testament. But our prayer is that, through reading about Hannah and uncovering her prophetic song that tells of Jesus, you are able to find yourself in this story, as well. In our waiting seasons, God is always at work and He will not leave us without hope. Let's close today by looking at the words of Lamentations 3:21-24 and asking Jesus to be our hope in the midst of whatever we are longing for today:

"But this I call to mind,

and therefore I have hope:

The steadfast love of the LORD never ceases;

his mercies never come to an end;

they are new every morning;

great is your faithfulness.

'The LORD is my portion,' says my soul,

'therefore I will hope in him.'"

PROPHECY FOUND IN POETRY

It's not breaking news that the Old Testament includes A LOT of different kings. We even saw evidence of kingship in Hannah's story yesterday. These books of the Bible in the Old Testament can feel confusing. Not only are there a lot of kings to keep straight, but there are also historical references that might feel unfamiliar to us in our culture today. But don't stress, friend — this is why we're going through this study together!

Today we find ourselves in Psalm 2. The heading of Psalm 2 in the ESV translation says "The Reign of the Lord's Anointed" and in the CSB translation it says "Coronation of the Son."

Lysa here. Just going to advocate for my everyday, Bible-reading friend and let you know that a coronation is "the ceremony of crowning a sovereign ruler." Carry on!

Psalm 2 is often referred to as a "coronation psalm" or a "royal psalm," and it's actually one of the most quoted psalms in the New Testament, as it's referenced at least 19 times. As we dig deeper into the text today, we'll see why, but first, let's talk about what happens during one of these "crowning ceremonies" and how people would have felt about it.

The coronation of the new king came with all the "ideals" this new kingship promised. A new king could bring better security, power, wealth and opportunity that may have been lacking in the previous king. This was important because most of the kings during this time were found untrustworthy and didn't live up to the standard of the "ideal" king people longed for.

This is why having an "ideal" other than God can be such a slippery slope. It's so very easy for these "ideals" to lead to large frustrations and ultimately letdowns because things and people will inevitably fail us.

Lysa here. I once did an Instagram live with my counselor, Jim Cress, when I was asking him about managing expectations. I had used the word "expectations" many times before he stopped me and asked me a pivotal question: "Lysa, do you know what expectations really are? Premeditated resentments." The more we set "ideal standards," the more we may be setting ourselves up to be disappointed. God had already warned the people that no human king would be "ideal."

Yikes. The frustrations we experience from having ideal expectations are the same feelings the people felt with these untrustworthy kings of Israel.

01 | Read Psalm 2:1-3. What are the kings of the nations doing?

02 | Continue reading Psalm 2:4-5 in the CSB translation. Psalm 2:4 describes a scene of God sitting on His throne in heaven, responding to the corruption and arrogance of the human rulers and kings mentioned in the previous verses. What is the response of the *"one enthroned"*?

We see revealed, right in the middle of the text, a prophetic song of a different kind of King. Not an untrustworthy, earthly king who would fail the people of Israel but an ever-faithful, eternal King who would soon save all people: King Jesus.

If you recall in our study of Hannah yesterday, we learned the Hebrew word מָשִׁיחַ *(mā·šîaḥ)*, translated as "anointed," is also the word for "Messiah."

03 | Go back and read Psalm 2:2. What word do you see again?

Yep, it's the same word. This psalmist is not just talking about an ideal human king but rather the expectation for the *"Anointed"* Son (Psalm 2:2) who is the King set on Mount Zion. (Psalm 2:6) The ESV Bible translation says He is *"begotten"* of the King, and He is enthroned in the heavens (Psalm 2:7b). This royal coronation song of Psalm 2 is a prophetic song of anticipation for the real King of kings: the Anointed One, none other than King Jesus. And because King Jesus is the ideal King, He can live up to the ideal standards no human king ever could. We can trust Him like no other leader because He will care for us and lead us like no other leader.

04 | How does this comfort you right now?

— A NOTE FROM JOEL

Mount Zion is an important location mentioned often throughout the Old Testament. Mount Zion is often referred to as and believed to be the place where God dwells and rules (see Isaiah 8:18). Sometimes, the temple is referred to as "Zion" or "Mt. Zion" or "the holy hill" because, again, the temple is where God would dwell (see Psalm 76:1-2). Zion is also sometimes referred to as the city that is on top of the mountain, that would be the future hope of the people of God and the place where God would rule and reign over the world. (Micah 4:7)

Let's look a little deeper into how this prophecy becomes even more real through specific examples of the life of Jesus.

- One of the most central themes of all of Scripture is not just kings or kingship but the Kingdom of God.[17] In the Old Testament, there is a constant picture of God as King. In the New Testament, Jesus' primary message, especially in the teachings of the Gospels, is the arrival of the *"kingdom of God"* because the King, Christ, entered human history by coming to earth and dwelling among us (Mark 1:14-15).

- This coronation psalm would actually have been sung or stated through multiple celebrations on a single day. But the coronation of Jesus took place repeatedly throughout His earthly ministry as the "Sonship" of Jesus was affirmed multiple times. God the Father addressed Jesus as "my son," and that's why Jesus is often referred to as the "Son of God."

05 | Read Matthew 3:17, Matthew 17:5, Acts 13:33 and Romans 1:14. What common phrase do you see in all of these verses?

We began today by reading about the many ways the ancient kings of Israel never measured up to who they were supposed to be. They couldn't live up to the "ideal" king the people longed for because ultimately they were just real people. Jesus was prophesied to us through the royal coronation song of Psalm 2. Therefore, we no longer need to seek after an "ideal" king because we now have the very best King in Jesus.

Jesus was really the Messiah.

Jesus was really the begotten Son of God.

Jesus "inherited" (reclaimed) the nations by His spilled blood on the cross, tearing down the dividing wall of hostility (Ephesians 2) and making those who were once enemies into brothers and sisters. He created reconciliation in a way that no earthly king could accomplish.

Jesus did conquer the enemies of God, but He did so by conquering sin, the devil and ultimately death through His own death, burial, resurrection and ascension.

The people of Israel LONGED FOR RESCUE, *but what they really* NEEDED WAS REDEMPTION.

Redemption is like the ultimate rescue because it grants us something we could never obtain on our own: freedom from sin and death. And only King Jesus could grant us this gift of redemption by forever conquering death by sacrificing His very own life.

What a beautiful picture. His sacrificial death brought us life.

Friend, whatever or whomever you may be looking to for rescue today, invite Jesus into that space right now. Open your hands right where you are and ask for His help and intervention. Colossians 1:13 says, *"He has delivered us from the domain of darkness and transferred us to the kingdom of his beloved Son."* Even when we aren't rescued from going through difficult circumstances, because of Jesus, redemption is always possible. His redemption means that evil will not have the final say in your story or mine.

As we continue to see Jesus in the Old Testament, I pray you not only begin to see Jesus in unexpected ways in your life right now but also see His love for you revealed from the very beginning of time.

PROPHECY FOUND IN THE MINOR PROPHETS

As we have studied different prophecies telling of Jesus in the Old Testament this week, remember that there are also sections of books in the Old Testament called "The Prophets" (see the introduction to this week for a refresh here!). These books are often split into two groups: the Minor Prophets and the Major Prophets. They're not called "minor" and "major" prophets because of their level of importance but rather their length of content. Today we are going to look into the book of Micah, one of the Minor Prophets.

Let's start by reading Micah 5:1-6. If you notice, in the ESV translation, this chapter is labeled as "The Ruler to Be Born in Bethlehem."

Micah 5:1-6 is sometimes referred to as an "oracle," or an announcement of hope. However, at this point in history, the audience would have been very skeptical of this. There was a long history where the Israelites could look back and see all their failures and the failures of the kings they had trusted. Easily, this would create skepticism in their hearts. The thought seemed too good to be true that they would have a ruler over Israel who would finally provide a way for them to live securely.

Most of the time, things that sound too good to be true on the front end turn out to be untrue on the back end. And because the Israelites found themselves once again in between a hard place (they had watched the northern kingdom of Israel fall to the Assyrians) and an even harder place (Micah prophesied of their own future judgment), they would have been tempted to feel skeptical as the prophet Micah spoke this grand announcement of hope.

01 | What is making you skeptical of God's good promises right now?

As we've previously mentioned, sometimes biblical prophecy has a bifocal nature. In Micah 5:1-6, we see this duality revealed, as Micah first casts a vision for an immediate future but also communicates an echo of what's to come.

Micah 5:1 says, *"Now muster your troops, O daughter of troops; siege is laid against us; with a rod they strike the judge of Israel on the cheek."*

Wow. While verses like this one can feel intimidating as you're trying to discern what Micah is really saying, don't worry — we're not going to leave you hanging in uncertainty.

In order to help us narrow down what is happening historically, scholars point out a few things in this verse. But before that, let's get on the same page about the kings being referenced here:

KING NEBUCHADNEZZAR:
A Babylonian king who destroyed Jerusalem and carried Judah into captivity.

KING ZEDEKIAH:
The last king of Judah.

- The *"siege"* in Micah 5:1 refers to King Nebuchadnezzar and his army that attacked Israel.[18]

- The *"judge of Israel"* also mentioned in verse 1 would be King Zedekiah, the last "ruler/judge" of Judah and therefore of "Israel."

- The significance of this judge of Israel being *"struck on the cheek"* with a rod could be a reference to any damage or harm that is done to the face. So King Zedekiah was figuratively "struck on the cheek," and in actuality, his eyes were gouged out.

- The *"rod"* comes from the Hebrew word שֵׁבֶט *(šēḇeṭ)* and can also be translated as "scepter," which also helps give context to the situation of Micah 5:1.[19] The scepter was a symbol that conveyed leadership, power and dominion. So what we find in Micah 5:1 is that the enemy of Israel would use the full weight of their military power against Israel. In a modern-day context, this would be like the president of the United States using the full weight of the military against an enemy of the U.S. We know the full weight of the military includes the Army, the Navy, the Air Force and the Marines.

Joel here. Read 2 Kings 25:7, Jeremiah 39:6-7 and Jeremiah 52:10-11 for more context here.

There's a lot happening here, and it's helpful for us to remember the historical context of the prophet Micah. All of these historical details prepare us to learn about another King, very different from King Zedekiah, who would also face attack and suffer in some similar ways.

02 | Read Matthew 27:30 and record the details of what's taking place.

03 | Read Mark 15:19 and record the details of what's taking place.

04 | Read John 19:3 and record the details of what's taking place.

We've already learned so much this week as we've seen how King Jesus is truly not just better than any Old Testament king, but He is the *ultimate* King. However, while He always reigned with complete authority and sovereignty, He was not spared suffering while on earth. Jesus had enemies just like any king would. He was struck by those with power (remember the "scepter"). These people included those in government (Pilate and Herod) and ruling leaders (Pharisees and Sadducees). And as Jesus was handed over for crucifixion, He was physically struck on the jaw.

This also takes us back to Day 6 this week in Genesis 3:15, where we uncovered that Jesus would be struck by the enemy, but in the end, Jesus would claim forever victory and reclaim His people from the grips of sin and death.

05 | How does hearing about the suffering and persecution of Jesus give you even greater insight that He understands the pain we're in when we walk through these things, too?

Micah didn't just prophesy of the Messiah, but he also provided some details surrounding who this Messiah would be and where He would come from. Take out your Bible and read Micah 5:2-6.

· MICAH 5:2

The fact that Micah clearly defines the location of the birth of the future King as *"Bethlehem Ephrathah"* is important. You see, there were at least two cities with the name Bethlehem. But Bethlehem Ephrathah was near Jerusalem while the other was in Zebulon. (Joshua 19:15)[20] Why is this so important? Because the prophecy of Micah is not generic but super specific. He zeroes in on a finite area. But not just any area — a small and distinct area that was the same Bethlehem as legendary King David's hometown (see 1 Samuel 16:1). This is a prophecy connecting back to the promise God made to David that someone from his lineage would always be on the throne of Israel. (2 Samuel 7:16)

MICAH 5:4

Verse 4a tells us this King will rule *"in the majesty of the name of the LORD [Yahweh] his God."* The connection to Jesus the Messiah is vital here. Jesus was the faithful Son of God, same in essence as the Father but distinct in person. He did not do things His own way or even according to His own will. Remember in the Old Testament the people referred to God as "Yahweh." So for Jesus to live, act and ultimately rule in the name of Yahweh was so special and unique. This was something only Jesus could do because Jesus Himself was Yahweh. (John 10:30)

What a beautiful mystery to try and wrap our minds around: the truth that Jesus is God and therefore all of His actions are a perfect reflection and representation of the character of God the Father. As one Old Testament scholar has said, "The fulfillment of these words is more marvelous than Micah's audience could have known."[21] Why is this so marvelous? Because in King Jesus, God gives them so much more than they could expect from an earthly king.

MICAH 5:5

The promise of this future King would result in the one thing that humanity had been longing for since Genesis 3 and the fall of creation: peace.

Let's look at the description of the peace that the Messiah would bring and how He would bring it. First, He Himself is Peace. Where Jesus went, peace followed because Jesus is peace. But notice what we're not saying here. Just because Jesus is peace doesn't mean there wasn't chaos, confusion or conflict that surrounded Him and the disciples. It does mean that, instead of waiting for the circumstances to get resolved and bring peace to Him, Jesus brought the peace in the middle of the circumstances.

What an incredible perspective. Since we've been working through this together, we have uncovered the consequences of sin and how much we have all suffered since the fall because of the cost of sin. One theologian describes sin as something that "disturbs shalom [peace]— twisting, weakening and snapping the thousands of bonds that give particular beings integrity and that tie them to others."[22]

Sin creates chaos and disrupts peace, and sin can only be made right through the cleansing work of Jesus and His shed blood. Because Jesus is the One who ties everything together, (John 1:1) when He enters the scene, He deals with sin through the cross. At the cross Jesus makes reconciliation and restoration possible. This means we can live with peace in our hearts because of Jesus.

Where we go, the peace of Jesus goes, and that should impact both people and creation.

This is one of the ways that Jesus brings peace in our life, and how we, too, can bring peace into hostile environments and situations in our life today. Because we belong to the Prince of Peace, who resides in us and works through us, we get to essentially be agents and ambassadors of peace.

06 | Where are you feeling desperate for peace in your own life right now? How do these truths encourage you?

Now that we know what Micah 5:2-6 is displaying, we can go back to Micah 5:1 with a fresh perspective when we consider how the Israelites would have heard these words with very little hope of them ever being true.

Today, we stand in the middle of hope, where we know with certainty Jesus came and at the same time we are waiting for Him to return. So what does this prophecy teach us to do in the meantime? Micah 5:1 tells us: Gather, prepare and eventually fight back against the siege.

Friend, the people of God are always given something to do while we wait for hope. We can gather as the family of God, pray, worship, serve our communities, share the encouraging Truth of Jesus and aim to be that brilliant light, like a city on a hill, that illuminates the darkness. (Matthew 5:16) Even while we wait for our hope to be made complete, we are not alone. And because God is not absent, we are not waiting in hopelessness but in hopeful anticipation.

MICAH 5:2-6	*OT* CONNECTIONS to Micah 5:2-6	*NT* CONNECTIONS to Micah 5:2-6
5:2 [1] Will come out of Bethlehem	Jeremiah 23:5; 30:21	Matthew 2:6; Luke 2:15; John 7:42
5:2 [1] Ruler in Israel	Isaiah 9:6-7; Jeremiah 30:21; 35:5	Matthew 27:11; Hebrews 1:3
5:2 [1] His origin is from before the days of old		John 1:1-3; 17:5; 1 John 1:1
5:2 [2] Will instigate a return of Israel	Isaiah 11:11-12; 49:5-6; Micah 7:14	Acts 1:6-7
5:2 [3] Stand and shepherd	Isaiah 11:3; 40:11; 42:1; Jeremiah 23:4-6	John 10:11; Hebrews 13:20; 1 Peter 4:4; Revelation 7:17
5:2 [3] In the strength and majesty of Yahweh	Isaiah 49:3; 5; 60:21	John 14:10; Hebrews 13:20
5:2 [3] He will be magnified in the earth	Psalm 110: Isaiah 9:6; 52:13	John 17:5; Acts 19:17; Hebrews 1:3; 8:1; 2 Peter 1:16
5:2 [4] He will be peace	Isaiah 9:6; 11:6-9	Ephesians 2:14; Colossians 1:20
5:2 [3] Shepherd with a sword	Isaiah 9:4-5; 49:2	Matthew 10:34; Revelation 1:16; 2:16; 19:15

Chart adapted from: JoAnna M. Hoyt, Amos, Jonah, & Micah, ed. H. Wayne House and William D. Barrick, Evangelical Exegetical Commentary (Bellingham, WA: Lexham Press, 2018), 725.

PROPHECY FOUND IN THE MESSIAH

Remember we started this week talking about how prophecy can include future events that are more immediate and others that are much further away. Today, we are going to study an Old Testament prophecy that promised that the Messiah (Jesus) would not only come, but when He came He would bring with Him justice and righteousness.

If you've watched the news lately, or scrolled on social media, you may have noticed most of the headlines aren't exactly uplifting. In fact, it seems like the things that are most absent in our world are justice and righteousness. Even a quick look in our history books shows that every generation has experienced heartache as a result of injustice in our communities, societies and world on this side of eternity. But probably most jarring of all is when we experience injustice personally in our homes, workplaces or even churches.

01 Whether it's something you've been made aware of on the news or something you've seen up close and personal, what injustice is breaking your heart right now?

When we look back at the Old Testament, we find that God has always cared about these issues. God's heart of special care for the oppressed and hurting is evidence of His great compassion and desire to see all people, from all nations, be welcomed into the family of God.

But like any healthy family we must deal with injustice, corruption and unrighteousness when we become aware of it.

This is why the prophecy of the coming Messiah in Isaiah 9:6-7 includes some details that we can't miss. The Messiah would bring with Him what was needed to deal with the hurt of the world.

6 "For to us a child is born,
to us a son is given;
and the government shall be upon his shoulder,
and his name shall be called
Wonderful Counselor, Mighty God,
Everlasting Father, Prince of Peace.
7 Of the increase of his government and of peace
there will be no end,
on the throne of David and over his kingdom,
to establish it and to uphold it
with justice and with righteousness
from this time forth and forevermore.
The zeal of the LORD of hosts will do this."

It's common to hear Isaiah 9:6 read aloud at Christmas. But sometimes verse 7 gets lost in the focus on verse 6. Keeping these verses together brings more context and power to them both.

Let's define two terms found in verse 7 so we have a common understanding of our foundation before diving in further. Those words are "justice" and "righteousness."

— A NOTE FROM JOEL

Another word that relates closely with righteousness is "uprightness," from the Hebrew word *"Me - Sha - Rim,"* which means conforming to a moral standard.

"Justice" comes from the Hebrew word *"mishpat"* and refers to a legal decision. "Righteousness" comes from the Hebrew word *"tsedeq,"* meaning rightness based on a standard.[24] This standard in the Old Testament is the Law. In the New Testament, the Law has been. written on our hearts, and the standard is Jesus, who lives up to every requirement of the Law. Jesus is the complete fulfillment of the Law

We see justice and righteousness fleshed out in two significant ways throughout the Old Testament:[25]

- First, God is just as He carries out the salvation He has promised in the Old Testament. We know this promise is true because of the New Testament that declares the Messiah is Jesus.
- Second, God in His righteousness responds to the oppression of those who are in affliction.

With these definitions and examples in mind, we can now see what Isaiah 9:6-7 prophesies about the Messiah.

These verses tell us a lot about Jesus.

It's also important to focus on the names associated with Jesus. Circle back to Isaiah 9:6.

02 | What words are used to describe the names of this "son"?

The way this verse is translated in English leaves us seeing these four phrases as a description: *"Wonderful Counselor, Mighty God, Everlasting Father, Prince of Peace"* (Isaiah 9:6).

But when we look at the way the Hebrew is actually written, we should really see only two thoughts written out as a sentence:

"[Wonderful Counselor, Mighty God], AND [Everlasting Father, Prince of Peace]."

Old Testament scholar John Goldingay does an excellent job translating the Hebrew phrases into full sentences for us to grasp the significance of these names. Goldingay reminds us these names and phrases are a definition for what the Messiah stands for.[26] The name, in a sense, makes a declaration about the character and substance of the person of Jesus the Messiah. You may be wondering why Jesus is called "Mighty God." Don't worry — as we study these two phrases we will explore one of the great mysteries of the Bible that we have already touched on throughout this study. Just remember: When we look at Jesus we are actually looking at the perfect imprint of the Father. This is why Jesus is called *"Mighty God."* Remember, man and woman are made in the image of God but only Jesus *is* the image of God. (Hebrews 1:3)

03 | Which of these names means the most to you right now and why?

So let's take a deeper look at these two phrases. Here's how we can understand the first phrase, *"Wonderful Counselor, Mighty God"*: [27]

The phrase combines two important thoughts. First, that Jesus is wonderful. But what is He wonderful at? The word "counselor" deals with planning and strategy. In the Hebrew language it has overtones of military planning. Think of a brilliant military general who makes plans and gives wise counsel. The third word speaks to the might of Jesus. Not only is Jesus able to plan and strategize in wonderful ways, but He is mighty to act out and accomplish everything that He plans. In other words, we are reminded that Jesus has a plan to reunite God's family that is divided because of injustice, lack of righteousness, hardship and the hurt that they have experienced.[28]

Wow. This gives us great confidence and assurance that God isn't just "winging it" or simply reacting to the events of history. No, He isn't caught off guard. Somehow, in a way that only He can, God is planning, directing and orchestrating history toward a final period of justice and righteousness.

And now let's take a look at how we can understand this phrase *"Everlasting Father, Prince of Peace"*:

This phrase suggests that the Messiah (Jesus) is the *"Everlasting Father,"* a striking claim that affirms His divine nature. The Father is also a *"Prince,"* who brings about shalom. Goldingay makes the observation, "In this context, shalom will then include the idea of peace, but the word commonly has the broader meaning of well-being — life as a whole going well."[29]

Lysa here. As I read this, I keep thinking how much I want and need all of who Jesus is in my life. And it gives me such comfort to know all that He brings to the afflictions we suffer and the injustices we can sometimes feel so helpless to face.

How will this all come about? Through the Messiah as He rules through justice and righteousness.

Isaiah 9:6 is commonly quoted around Christmastime as we celebrate the birth of the long-awaited Messiah, but it's incredible how God still fulfills these things in our world today. In the times of Scripture, Jesus fulfilled this assignment, but now we get the opportunity to participate in His justice and righteousness.

Let's finish today by looking at some verses about how we can do this:

04 | Read Matthew 5:6 and Matthew 6:33. What stands out to you?

05 | Go to the book of James and look at the following verses: James 1:9-10; 2:1-10; 5:1-6. Meditate on the verses that stand out to you and jot down some personal takeaways.

As we close this week's study, let's pray together. *Father God, thank You for the truths we unpacked this week in Your Word. I praise You for these revelations You are showing me while I find myself in my own waiting place. I pray right now that You would strengthen my faith today. Show me more of You. And thank You for Your Son, Jesus. He is evidence that reminds me You always keep Your promises. Continue to show me more of Him in the coming weeks of this study. In Jesus' Name, Amen.*

WEEK
three

WELCOME TO WEEK 3, FRIEND.

If you're reading this, it means you made it through trying to wrap your mind around all those Old Testament prophecies ... You are practically a Bible scholar now!

This week, we are diving into our third category of how we can see Jesus in the Old Testament: *patterns*.

Patterns are everywhere in Scripture, but in the Old Testament particularly, the earliest patterns are found in Genesis 1-3. Though we've already studied Adam and Eve and the Garden of Eden during this study, let's point out something we haven't focused on yet: the pattern of God and the pattern of the enemy.

Let's first look at the pattern of God from the creation story (Genesis 1-2):

- God plants a **beautiful** garden ...
- God fills up that garden with **beautiful** things ...
- God creates the most **beautiful** and unique creation of all, humanity.

God **creates.** What God **creates is good** and beautiful. And God appoints **His good creation** to multiply and fill the earth with evidence of His goodness and glory. (Genesis 1:28b) The pattern here is that anything God creates is beautiful and such a brilliant reflection of Himself.

This brings us to the pattern of the serpent, who we know is our enemy, Satan. The enemy's pattern is to separate people from God, from God's beautiful and best plans, and from their fellow humans. As a matter of fact, Satan's name in Hebrew means to oppose, obstruct or accuse. The Greek word literally means "adversary."[30] So that's his pattern. He creates opposition, obstruction and accusation all in order to turn us into adversaries. Remember, on Day 3 and Day 6 of this study we've already looked at John 10:10, which shows the extreme measures Satan will take to separate us from God and from one another: He will steal, kill and destroy.

The serpent tempts Adam and Eve to go against God's instructions by enticing them to think that if they eat from the tree of the knowledge of good and evil, they won't die but instead *"will be like God"* (Genesis 3:5). The irony and tragedy of this story is that God had *already* made Adam and Eve in His image. They were already like God.

Don't miss this. *They were already like God.* And when they took the bait of the enemy, he lured them away from being like God. So, in sinning, Adam and Eve got the exact opposite of the outcome they had hoped for. God's plan for good was not only interrupted, but separation between God and His creation was present for the very first time.

God's pattern is to bring about good.

The enemy's pattern is to bring about evil.

The pattern of humans is wanting good but continuing to sin, which disrupts God's plan for good.

Despite the human pattern of sin, God doesn't pivot His plans for good. God doesn't leave things broken. Even though separation was created, it would not be permanent.

God would send a Rescuer. And though the heel of this promised Rescuer would be bruised, eventually, the head of the enemy would be crushed. (See Genesis 3:15 or Week 2, Day 6 of this study.)

How incredible is that? Though God's original pattern was interrupted by sin, God set a new pattern into motion.

- God promises good to humanity ...
- Humanity responds with rebellion and breaks relationship with God ...
- God promises that the relationship will not be broken forever, but the path to reunion will include pain ...
- Jesus endures this pain, conquers evil, pays the price for humanity's sin, and restores the possibility of a relationship between God and humanity.

So, with Jesus, the pattern we see is one of *redemptive reversals*. Jesus is the redeemer of all things. But we can especially see this in His reversing the effects of sin and starting the process of redemption, even in the Old Testament, by restoring mankind back to God's best. Be sure to put some thought into the questions this week so you can see how the pattern of humans turning away from God, since the beginning of time, is often repeated in our lives as well. But the great news is that Jesus' pattern to redeem and reverse has been evident throughout history and is very much still active in our lives, too. This week, we will look for Jesus as we study the patterns of famine and rain, falling and rising, wilderness and promised land, less-than and greater-than, and chaos and order.

Jesus is the hope of these redemptive reversals and the new pattern God the Father put into motion. We will see the hope in what's harsh, the new life in what's nearly dead, and the possibilities in what may look impossible.

Our redeemer lived. Our redeemer lives. Nothing is beyond His ability to reverse. What a great comfort that is!

THE PATTERN OF FAMINE AND RAIN

Do you ever look around at all that is happening in our world today and feel fear grip your heart?

We crave safety and certainty and simplicity as we raise our families, serve God and live out our Christian beliefs. But so many things feel threatening to those desires.

Whether it's something we're facing right now or something we fear will happen in the future, fear can seem so consuming.

01 | What are you feeling afraid of right now?

For the Israelites, the number one thing they feared the most and did not want in their land was *famine*. Famine meant sure death because the rainwaters ceased or were very scarce. The Israelites were primarily farmers, and their livelihood depended on the rainfall to produce crops. Without rain, circumstances were dire and devastation was certain.

02 What do the following verses also teach us about the importance of rain?

Leviticus 26:4

Deuteronomy 28:12

Ezekiel 34:26

The pattern of rain and famine was this: Where there was rain, there was a fear that famine would return. Where there was famine, there was a desperation for rain. Before we go further into famine and rain and how these connect to Jesus, there are a few more details about the rain that will be helpful to know.

03 Read Deuteronomy 11:14, Psalm 84:6 and James 5:7. What are the two kinds of rain we discover in these verses?

— A NOTE FROM JOEL

The early rain, also known as the autumn rain, would come in September or October. Almost 75% of rain for the Israelites would fall between December and February. The late rain, or spring rain, would come between March and May and would be the rainfall that actually caused the crops to ripen.[31]

Though a lack of rain may not be what you are facing today, we all have fears. And when fear begins to consume us we will reach for anything that can help us regain a sense of control. Though it may be harder to identify when this is happening in the midst of our own fears, we can see this clearly in the way the Israelites began to react. Only God could provide rain or keep rain back from them. This is why the Israelites may have been tempted to worship and follow Baal, the Canaanite thunder/storm god. They felt they couldn't control God so they stopped trusting Him.

04 | Let that sentence sit with you for just a minute. Is there a part of you that can relate to the Israelites here?

Lysa here. Time for another confession on my part ... I can often catch myself thinking I don't have much in common with the children of Israel, but in all honesty, I do. If God doesn't do what I thought He would, I'm tempted to try and figure things out on my own rather than trust Him. I pray, but then I keep trying to fix what's beyond my ability to fix. Especially when I'm afraid, my prayers sometimes start to sound more like me giving instructions to God rather than taking instructions from God.

The Israelites were so afraid of famine they started trying to work on getting rain for themselves. They looked at what the pagan countries around them were doing and started worshipping and sacrificing to false gods that represented weather, rain, fertility and more. They took "control" by trying to win the favor of the pagan gods, which made them feel less vulnerable. But this distrust of God made them disobedient to God. After all, God had made it very clear to the Israelites that they were to have no other gods besides Him.

So how could they justify this? David Guzik explains that "Israel considered their idolatry and sacrifice to pagan gods to be of little consequence. Many of them probably told themselves that they were not forsaking the Lord, only adding the worship of these other gods." But they were wrong, and taking things into their own hands would backfire on them.

05 | Read Jeremiah 3:2-3 and Amos 4:7-8. What was the reason behind God withholding rain in these verses?

David Guzik later says, "Spiritually, Israel's idolatry polluted the land — therefore God withheld the rain they needed for crops and food. This had special irony, because many of the pagan gods they went after were associated with weather, rain and fertility (such as Baal and Ashtoreth)."[32] So what happens when the rains are withheld? *Famine.*

Let's not miss this important detail. In an effort to prevent a famine, the Israelites wound up causing one. They downplayed their disobedience. They refused to recognize that turning away from God was the same as choosing to turn toward sin. And the drought in their spiritual lives led to a drought in their physical lives. This is where we will see the redemptive reversal of Jesus. He takes humanity's deep physical desire for water and uses it to reveal an even more crucial soul need for Living Water. Then, He doesn't just reveal our need — He becomes the conduit through which the redemptive Living Water of God comes to us.

But first, now that we've seen how this fear of famine played out in a nation of people, let's see how it played out with an individual. To do that, we'll take another look at the life of King David.

There was once a situation where David disobeyed God by taking a census he was instructed not to take. Turn to 2 Samuel 24:1-14 to read more. Because sin always comes as a package deal, this act of disobedience would unleash punishment. God allowed David to choose between famine, war or pestilence as a punishment. David chose pestilence, a deadly and overwhelming disease that would impact his entire community. Though David feared the choice of a famine more, make no mistake: Pestilence came with a severe cost to the people. Over 70,000 men died during the three days of the deadly disease. (2 Samuel 24:15)

Here's another important connection I want us to make. The disobedience of David resulted in three days of death for many people. The three days here in David's story point to another three-day time period in the life of Jesus where we see Him revealed as the Redeemer. The obedience of Jesus resulted in His own death for a period of three days, after which He would provide a way to redeem people plagued with sin to help them find new life. He reverses the finality of death and brings the possibility for new life. Philippians 2:8 speaks to this incredible revelation of Jesus' pattern of reversal: *"And being found in human form, he humbled himself by becoming obedient to the point of death, even death on a cross. Therefore God has highly exalted him and bestowed on him the name that is above every name, so that at the name of Jesus every knee should bow, in heaven and on earth and under the earth, and every tongue confess that Jesus Christ is Lord, to the glory of God the Father"* (Philippians 2:8-11).

Jesus took on the PUNISHMENT OF DEATH for our sins to REVERSE THE CURSE of us being *eternally separated* from God.

06 | Has there been a time in your life where you know you acknowledged the redemption of Jesus as something you need and accepted the gift of salvation He has offered? Write about your experience here or write about your desire to know more. If you want to read more about receiving new life from Jesus, go to page 193 in the back of this study guide to be led through a prayer of salvation.

While we've been learning about a physical famine of the earth, there is also a spiritual famine and drought (lack of rain) that humanity has been plagued with because of sin. Biblical authors would often use common, everyday language and examples from their period of time to talk about spiritual situations they wanted to convey, and this topic of famine and rain is one example of that.

07 | Read Psalm 63:1. What connection do you see between famine and rain in the words of the psalmist?

Notice who this psalm is attributed to ... (Hint: Read the little subscript under the chapter heading to find this.)

King David.

Here we find David reflecting on a famine he experienced earlier in his life that probably fed his great fear of famines. He knew what it was like to search for water only to find more dust and greater thirst. David compares his deep desire for God to a persistent thirst. The reason for the thirst is attributed to *"a dry and weary land where there is no water,"* which is another way of describing a famine (Psalm 63:1).

David knew the ache of physical thirst and longing. But David also knew the deep ache of spiritual thirst.

Maybe you feel like David in your own way today. Maybe you're facing your own situation that you can't change no matter how much you do ... and you're still left *thirsty.*

If you're in this place, you're not alone, and you're not disqualified from having a real encounter with Jesus. Where you feel empty is an exact appointment to experience true Living Water. In fact, Jesus Himself tells us this.

John 7:37-38 says, *"On the last day of the feast, the great day, Jesus stood up and cried out, 'If anyone thirsts, let him come to me and drink. Whoever believes in me, as the Scripture has said, "Out of his heart will flow rivers of living water."'"*

Jesus even says in John 4:14 that *"... whoever drinks of the water that I will give him will never be thirsty again. The water that I will give him will become in him a spring of water welling up to eternal life."*

What we're really thirsting for is the Living Water that Jesus brings.

Now read Amos 8:11-12. Here, Scripture is helping us understand a famine that's even more extreme than physical famine. It's talking about a spiritual famine. Many people are emotionally and spiritually dying of soul starvation and thirst because they need the Word of God. They may have physical access to God's Word, but there's a big difference between physical access and personal access. Just because most of our homes have a couple of Bibles in them doesn't mean we are personally accessing the Scriptures and nourishing our souls.

But instead of going to God and turning to His Word, sometimes we try to seek satisfaction from solutions of our own making. We keep trying to quench that deep-soul thirst with people, possessions, positions and platforms. The problem is, while some of these things can make us feel happy for a season, they will all eventually make us desperately empty and thirsty (like a famine) if we don't have the Lord. Only He can quench the deep longings of our soul.

As we close today, let's read Jeremiah 2:11-13:

"Has a nation changed its gods,
even though they are no gods?
But my people have changed their glory
for that which does not profit.
Be appalled, O heavens, at this;
be shocked, be utterly desolate,
declares the LORD,
for my people have committed two evils:
they have forsaken me,
the fountain of living waters,
and hewed out cisterns for themselves,
broken cisterns that can hold no water."

Oh, friends. Our souls are tailor-made to be filled with Jesus and His Truth. That means nothing else will be able to seep into every part of us. Nothing else will be able to refresh, restore and transform us. Nothing else will ever truly satisfy our souls. None of those solutions or idols we reach for in desperate need for control will bring us lasting satisfaction and peace.

Physical famine continues to be a real problem for areas of our world, and as Christians we should care deeply for those in need. However, for most of us today, we deal with a famine of the soul. But we don't have to fear this kind of famine because we have a spring of Eternal Water that is accessible to us every day, every moment of our lives. This is possible because we have Jesus' gift of the Holy Spirit who gives us spiritual water and satisfies the deep longing and thirst of the human spirit. (John 7:38-39)[33]

Do you see how these verses are connecting the Old Testament and the New Testament? All of this is coming together for us to be reminded our souls have a real hunger and thirst that God created in us. But those longings don't have to be just desperations for us IF we remember every longing is a reminder for us to look to Jesus as the only real way to access God's Living Water. And like Jesus preaches in Matthew 5:6, *"Blessed are those who hunger and thirst for righteousness, for they will be filled"* (NIV).

Dehydration starts *before* we are thirsty. That's why it's important to pay attention to what we fear and where we seek satisfaction and comfort. Before we shake our finger at the Israelites and their idolatry, let's close today by looking within ourselves. Write a prayer releasing your fears and instead turning to Jesus, who can reverse the negative effects of our fears and turn them into redemptive realities we may have never considered before.

Today I release ...

VARIOUS *famines* IN THE BIBLE

Abraham and Isaac migrate to escape famine. Where do they go? Egypt. Here we see a pattern: As a result of the seven-year famine, Jacob and his family live in ... EGYPT! (Genesis 41:57; Genesis 45:5-7; compare Acts 7:11)

PATRIARCHAL PERIOD *(Genesis 12:10; Genesis 26:1)*

Ruth and Elimilech migrate to Moab because of famine. (Ruth 1:1)

PRE-MONARCHIC *(before kings)*

Elijah, on behalf of God, initiates a three-year famine in the time of King Ahab. (1 Kings 17:1; 1 Kings 18:1-2; compare Luke 4:25) There is also a seven-year famine during the lifetime of Elisha. (2 Kings 4:38; 2 Kings 8:1)

MONARCHIC *(time of the kings)*

Haggai talks about a famine during the time of the Persians. (Haggai 1:10-11; Haggai 2:16) Nehemiah 5 records a famine.

POSTEXILIC *(after the exile)*

In Acts, Agabus prophesies of a famine that most likely took place during the time of the emperor Claudius (AD 41-54) and is referred to in extra-biblical sources. (Tacitus, Annals 12.43)

NEW TESTAMENT

THE PATTERN OF RISING AND FALLING

Have you ever cried over something so much that you truly feel like you've run out of tears? Your eyes are swollen and red while a current of unrest still rages through your soul. And you look up toward heaven in utter confusion ... "God, why aren't You doing something?"

Why aren't You answering my prayer?
Why aren't You intervening in this hopeless situation?
Why are You allowing this to happen?
Why, God?

01 | Which one of these questions do you find yourself saying out loud to God or to yourself? If it's a different question than one listed above, include that.

Earlier, in Week 2, we studied Hannah's story of heartbreak as she longed for a child. We learned her suffering eventually turned into song when God blessed her with a baby. But if anyone knew what it felt like to run out of tears because of a situation in which she was so powerless, it was Hannah.

This is the crux of one of the hardest parts about following God ... You know He is all-powerful and can literally do anything, but it's devastating when He is not demonstrating His power through the things you are begging Him for most.

02 | How do you resonate with these feelings in your life right now?

When we are in this place of long-suffering, the rollercoaster of emotions can seem all too real and leave us feeling vulnerable. One minute we're determined to trust God. And in the next, we can feel ourselves slipping. The "why?" questions tumble in so hard. The "worst-case scenarios" feel too real. And many times, our unanswered prayers leave us feeling like we keep hitting a *detour* instead of our intended destination.

Detours that go on for too long can begin to feel more like dead ends. What we thought was a pause turns into a screeching halt.

Whenever thinking about detours, the story of Joseph immediately comes to mind. We encounter the story of Joseph starting in Genesis 37. While we don't have the time to dive into his entire story today, there's no denying there are many parts of Joseph's story that didn't just feel like a detour but an actual reversal of the direction he thought his life would go ... There were long stretches of time when it must have felt like God was doing nothing. And we might have similar feelings when it seems we've hit a dead end and nothing looks like we expected:

That prayer will never be answered ...
The relationship we've dreamed of will never be reality ...
The dream of doing ministry will never happen ...
The pain will never go away ...
The healing won't be possible ...
The false accusations against us will never be righted ...
The hard circumstances will never get better ...

03 | If you find yourself in a detour situation that feels like a dead end, what are some of the lies you're tempted to believe? Confess some of these and begin to open your heart to what God may want to show you today. Write your thoughts below.

There are some details in Joseph's journey that reveal God is still with us even when we feel like we are falling behind, stuck in detours and derailed from the plan we envisioned for our life. Even when we fall, we will eventually rise. Detours and dead ends may be a part of our story, but they're never the whole story. We see the evidence of this truth revealed through Joseph.

There are many parts of Joseph's life where he temporarily falls back into what feels like a detour, but then he eventually rises. Here, we see a pattern of rising and falling. Let's take a look at some of these events:

- Joseph has a dream that his family will bow down to him (rising).
- Joseph is stripped of his clothes and thrown into a pit (falling … literally!).
- Joseph is sold into slavery but finds a position of honor in Potiphar's house (rising).
- Joseph acts with integrity and honor and refuses the sexual advances of Potiphar's wife, but this refusal lands him in prison (falling).
- Joseph gains leadership opportunities and even becomes friends with the cupbearer and baker in the prison, where he later interprets their dreams. As a result, Joseph is later called upon to interpret Pharaoh's dreams and is exalted into a position of high honor, second in power only to Pharaoh himself (rising).

How could you be thrown into a pit by your family, sold into slavery and then unfairly imprisoned without looking at God and asking "why?" Even though we've identified parts of Joseph's story that contain this pattern of rising and falling, Joseph's *falls* were not just little bumps in the road. And the *rising* moments did not feel like instant relief. No, there were stretches of time in between these rising and falling events.

— A NOTE FROM LYSA

The backstory of all these "falling" occurrences is actually where we eventually find the famous words of Genesis 50:20: *"You intended to harm me, but God intended it for good to accomplish what is now being done, the saving of many lives"* (NIV).

04 | Reflect on some of the details of Joseph's story. What stands out to you?

God had a plan. And his brothers' betrayal was not the end of Joseph's story. From the pit to the palace, Joseph was eventually positioned to spare the lives of his family and the entire nation of Israel.

This rising and falling pattern doesn't just apply to Joseph. We actually see the same pattern revealed in Jesus' life. Let's take a look ...

- Jesus condescends onto earth (falling).
  Joel here. "Condescension" is a theological term that refers to the incarnation of Christ, specifically that Christ "came down" from heaven onto the earth. The emphasis is placed on the "coming down." So when we mention "falling," this is to highlight moments where God "stooped" for us, in love. "Rising," on the other hand, highlights clear moments of victory.
- Jesus is baptized and affirmed by God the Father (rising).
- Jesus is led by the Spirit into the wilderness (falling).
- Jesus enters the city of Jerusalem in His triumphal entry (rising).
- Jesus embarks on the journey to the cross and crucifixion (falling).
- Jesus rises from the grave, conquering sin and death on the third day (rising).

04 | How is this pattern of *falling and rising* allowing you to see the story of Jesus in a new light today?

The tension between the falling and rising we see in the lives of Joseph and even Jesus can often create what look like detours and dead ends. But through the examples of Joseph and Jesus, we see another redemptive reversal: *Good* is where God leads us. Even when what we're experiencing right now doesn't feel good, we can trust that, no matter what, God never derails from His plan of eventual good ... in His way, in His timing.

There may be situations, circumstances, diagnoses and outcomes that don't reveal any evidence of good in the moment, but the truth is that God's story for us never just stops at a dead end. Romans 8:28 reminds us of this: *"And we know that for those who love God all things work together for good, for those who are called according to his purpose."*

And we pray, as you reflect further on the evidence of this in Scripture, you are even more encouraged by how faithful God is to us. He was working for good in the suffering of Joseph. He was working for good in the suffering of Jesus. And the same is true for us. But even better because we have the assurance of the ultimate good Jesus made a way for us to experience in eternity.

This leads us to another pattern we will study next: the in-between places of our lives that look like wilderness experiences or even seasons. Tomorrow we will study the wilderness and promised land.

DAY THIRTEEN

THE PATTERN OF WILDERNESS & PROMISED LAND

Joel here. I don't know about you guys, but the older I get and the more my family grows, every time we have to move, the stress level definitely rises! My wife, Brittany, and I have lived in four different cities, and we've moved cross-country more than once. When we moved to Charlotte, we moved into a house that we thought was perfect for us and our three boys. We thought for sure this was going to be our "forever home." Then, on Valentine's Day of 2021, we welcomed our baby girl, Emelia Jane (EmJ). We knew pretty soon that we were looking at another move and honestly it was really terrifying. We loved our neighborhood, and our kids loved their school, but we knew what we needed to do. The housing market was pretty crazy so we realized we were going to have to sell our house before we could even look at where we may move to. We made the decision to move forward but it left us feeling like we were in the middle of the wilderness. We had no idea where our new home would be, where our kids would go to school, and no clue how long this uncertainty was going to last. I think this feeling of being stuck may be something we can all relate to. It was definitely a feeling that the Israelites knew all too well.

Earlier, in Week 1, we looked into the lives of Moses and Joshua. During that study, we touched on the Israelites' journey from the wilderness to the promised land. And while this journey is a pivotal story in the Old Testament, it also represents a deeper pattern we can trace all the way to Jesus.

Throughout the Old Testament, the people of God found themselves in perpetual cycles of wilderness or desert experiences, with small glimpses of what the promised land would be like.

There are multiple Hebrew words (*midbār, yešîmôn, tōhû*) that translate into "desert," "wilderness" or "wasteland."[34] In fact, Genesis 1:2 says, *"The earth was without form [tōhû] and void ..."* showing us the very first picture of this concept. The world was void and darkness was present before God began creating the beauty of Eden and eventually His image bearers, Adam and Eve. In other words, the world was a wilderness or wasteland.

Let's pause here to consider something. What makes something a *wilderness*? There is the physical experience of a wilderness where the Israelites wandered, but there's also a spiritual experience. A spiritual wilderness can *feel like* the **absence of God.** It is feeling alone and hidden in suffering for an extended period of time. You know God is there, but you don't feel Him at all.

01 | Can you recall a time when you felt this way? What made something feel like a wilderness season to you?

And what makes something the *promised land?* It is evidence of the **presence of God.** Again, for the Israelites, this would have been an actual place where they ventured. For us, it spiritually symbolizes the fruitfulness of God. Maybe we have received answered prayers, breakthroughs in situations, or even just a season marked by close intimacy with God. It's a time when you hear Him more clearly than you have before. In other words, it's a place where His presence feels present. Hold on to these perspectives of both wilderness and promised land as we continue to study.

let's *trace this* pattern throughout scripture

The earth is void, dark and filled with chaos. (Genesis 1:1-2)	WILDERNESS
God plants a beautiful garden and places Adam and Eve in the garden to care for, keep and tend to it. (Genesis 2:15)	PROMISED LAND
Adam and Eve are cast out of Eden. (Genesis 3:23) God saves Noah and re-creates the earth to start over. (Genesis 6-9)	WILDERNESS
The people gather in the plains of Shinar (Babylon) and build a tower in rebellion against God. They are punished and dispersed. (Genesis 11:1-9)	PROMISED LAND
From the epicenter of rebellion (Ur of the Chaldeans/Babel), God calls Abraham and takes him to a new land. (Genesis 12:1-9)	WILDERNESS
Abraham's descendants experience famine and go to Egypt for safety. (Genesis 42)	FALSE PROMISED LAND → WILDERNESS
God rescues the Israelites out of Egypt. (Exodus 12-14)	PROMISED LAND
The Israelites sin and end up wandering in the wilderness for 40 years. (Exodus 16:35)	WILDERNESS
The Israelites, led by Joshua, enter the promised land. (Joshua 3)	PROMISED LAND
Israel eventually becomes a united kingdom under Saul and David. (1 Samuel 10; 2 Samuel 5:3)	PROMISED LAND
After Solomon's reign, the united kingdom is divided. (1 Kings 12:16-24)	WILDERNESS
Eventually Israel will be taken over by Assyria, Babylon and Persia and subjugated under oppressive Roman rule. (Isaiah 7:18; 2 Chronicles 36:17-21; Daniel 5:28-31; Luke 2:1-5)	WILDERNESS → EXILE

This pattern is repeated in so many places of Scripture. Though we can identify these different examples of wilderness to promised land, the bigger questions are: What does God want to teach us in both of these places, and what does He reveal about Jesus through them?

First, let's review how the wilderness journey began for the Israelites. Because of a famine, Jacob and his sons fled to Egypt. Egypt held the promise of prosperity, protection and provision, but in a terrible irony, it became the Israelites' prison. While in Egypt, the Israelites grew in number, and they were perceived as a threat by a pharaoh who did not know of Joseph. Because he feared the massive numbers of the Israelites, this new pharaoh forced them into slavery.

Pharaoh finally released the Israelites from their enslavement in Egypt, but look where they're sent next in Exodus 13:17-18: *"When Pharaoh let the people go, God did not lead them by way of the land of the Philistines, although that was near. For God said, 'Lest the people change their minds when they see war and return to Egypt.' But God led the people around by the way of the **wilderness** toward the Red Sea. And the people of Israel went up out of the land of Egypt equipped for battle"* (emphasis added).

The road towards the Philistines would have been the shortest, but God intentionally took Israel through the wilderness toward the Red Sea. Friend, even if we find ourselves in a wilderness kind of season, be encouraged today that, if God is allowing it, He will use it. The wilderness may be a place marked by desperation, drought, devastation and desolation, but God led the Israelites through it. And we can trust He will do the same for us.

02 | Read Deuteronomy 8:1-10 below. Underline any mention of wilderness, promised land and evidence of God's faithful activity:

"The whole commandment that I command you today you shall be careful to do, that you may live and multiply, and go in and possess the land that the LORD swore to give to your fathers. And you shall remember the whole way that the LORD your God has led you these forty years in the wilderness, that he might humble you, testing you to know what was in your heart, whether you would keep his commandments or not. And he humbled you and let you hunger and fed you with manna, which you did not know, nor did your fathers know, that he might make you know that man does not live by bread alone, but man lives by every word that comes from the mouth of the LORD. Your clothing did not wear out on you and your foot did not swell these forty years. Know then in your heart that, as a man disciplines his son, the LORD your God disciplines you. So you shall keep the commandments of the LORD your God by walking in his ways and by fearing him. For the LORD your God is bringing you into a good land, a land of brooks of water, of fountains and springs, flowing out in the valleys and hills, a land of wheat and barley, of vines and fig trees and pomegranates, a land of olive trees and honey, a land in which you will eat bread without scarcity, in which you will lack nothing, a land whose stones are iron, and out of whose hills you can dig copper. And you shall eat and be full, and you shall bless the LORD your God for the good land he has given you."

Let's go to one more place in Deuteronomy. Go to Deuteronomy 32:10-11.

03 | Record how Deuteronomy 32:10 describes the two places where God "found" Israel.

God found Israel in the *"desert land"* (*miḏbār*), but also in the *"howling waste of the wilderness"* (*yešîmôn*). These two words are used to describe the wasteland reality the Israelites experienced, but the double reference reinforces the severity of their situation.

— A NOTE FROM JOEL

Old Testament scholars are divided on exactly where Israel was at this time. Some scholars believe the reference is to Egyptian captivity that was a wilderness experience.[35] Others believe that the reference is to "Sinai." This was the desert area near Mount Sinai (Exodus 19:1-2) where the Israelites wandered for 40 years before entering the promised land.[36] This was also the place where Israel camped as they built the tabernacle. (Exodus 25-40) It may be that the double wilderness language connects to both experiences. Regardless of the reference to one or both situations, the presence and activity of God is the same.

In Deuteronomy 32:10-12, we see God caring for His people in their wilderness experience through three different metaphors:

Protector
The language reflects a protective eagle circling her children, keeping them within a "bird's eye" view. The imagery also tells us something about how God protects. He doesn't hover or smother but rather allows a degree of trust for His children to live with independence, but close enough for Him to intervene if danger should arrive.

We will actually spend a whole week on this topic of protection, but for now, let's look at a few verses:

"Many are the sorrows of the wicked, but steadfast love surrounds the one who trusts in the LORD." (Psalm 32:10)

"Keep me as the apple of your eye; hide me in the shadow of your wings ..." (Psalm 17:8)

"I will instruct you and teach you in the way you should go; I will counsel you with my eye upon you." (Psalm 32:8)

04 | Which of the three verses above seems to apply to something you are facing right now?

Teacher

The imagery of a teacher in Deuteronomy 32:10-12 is reflected by an eagle teaching its babies to fly. Sometimes the mother will push the eaglet out of the nest, letting it fall almost 90 feet. Then the mother swoops down and stabilizes the little bird by placing her wing under the baby for support. Then she soars to the top of the nest and repeats this process, letting the baby bird fall to depths of almost 150 feet.[37]

God teaches us in a similar fashion. He gives us freedom to make decisions, but He is always near us to provide guidance if we need it. Sometimes we wish God would just give us the solutions or answers to our problems and questions. But if you think about God being our teacher, just like in school, teachers never give you a cheat sheet. They equip you and empower you to take the test on your own. It may be more convenient if God gave us all the answers in the short-run. But in the long-run, His nature of guiding us, not micromanaging or forcing us, leads to growth inside of us and ultimately trust between us and God. Read Psalm 32:8 for more on this *teacher* portion.

Leader

God is pictured here as a hands-on, caring leader. (Deuteronomy 32:10-12) God does not leave His children to wander aimlessly but shows the right path forward, providing the necessary support and help. This is almost like combining His role of protector and teacher into one role as our leader. Leaders fiercely and faithfully protect, but they also provide vision for the future steps ahead and guidance and wisdom to get there.

Take a look at the words of 2 Thessalonians 3:3-5:

"But the Lord is faithful. He will establish you and guard you against the evil one. And we have confidence in the Lord about you, that you are doing and will do the things that we command. May the Lord direct your hearts to the love of God and to the steadfastness of Christ."

05 | Between these three roles, which one are you seeing God fulfill for you most specifically right now?

Just as God cared for the Israelites in their wilderness journey, He will do the same for us when we find ourselves in wilderness places.

In addition to the Israelites, let's close today by looking at one more person who knew the desolate places and feelings of the wilderness all too well: Jesus.

- As a child, Jesus had a wilderness type of experience as His family escaped to Egypt in hiding. (Matthew 2:13-15)
- Jesus was led into the wilderness by the Spirit (Matthew 4:1) and was tempted.

The same experiences the ancient Israelites had in the wilderness, Jesus also had.
Moses was sent to be the Israelites' in-person protector, teacher and leader through the journey of the wilderness. Moses was used by God to care for the people of God. But with Jesus, we see God *Himself* journeying through the wilderness and coming out on the other side as our protector, teacher and leader.

Because of Jesus, even though we feel we are far from the promised land, we can always live with the *promise* that He deeply understands, cares and will never leave us to figure it out on our own.

He will protect us in these places.
He will teach us in these places.
He will lead us through these places.

Jesus, and ultimately the Holy Spirit, as well, bridges the gap between the wilderness we're experiencing and the promised land we long for. Jesus is God's promise kept to us that, no matter what we're walking through, He will never be absent, and we will never be alone. Even when we don't feel it, God's presence is always present.

THE PATTERN OF LESS-THAN AND GREATER-THAN

Lysa here. A few weeks ago I sat in a pink dress on the sand and stared at the ocean. It was supposed to be a day of celebration. I'd gotten dressed up and took extra time doing my hair. I picked out just the right shade of lipstick and put a few essentials in a tiny purse that I don't use very often.

But only a few hours later, I was alone. A family member who was supposed to be there for me didn't show up. And now my hair was a wind-blown mess and most of my makeup had been wiped off. I stared out at the ocean and felt so small. The question that just kept nagging at me was, "Why don't things work out for me the way they seem to for other people?"

Earlier that night I'd been surrounded by people who all had someone by their side. I smiled and nodded my way through all the pleasantries required. I pretended to be interested in all the different conversations around me, but my mind wasn't really there.

And as soon as possible, I slipped outside to be by myself. I took my shoes off and walked far enough away so no one could hear me crying. I didn't want to be alone. But I didn't want to be with people either.

Rejection can make you feel like you don't belong anywhere. *God, I just don't know if I have it in me to believe any of this will ever be used for good. I don't know how to process this. I always thought You were going to use this pain for some significant plan. Now, I just feel like it's all pointless.*

There hasn't been enough time that's passed since that story happened to bring it all around with some big, spiritual lesson. No, it's still just fresh pain for me. And there's nothing to make it more tidy or less rattling. The only thing I keep reminding myself of right now is the upside-down nature of God.

He has a pattern of taking what makes us feel less-than and using it for great things. And then the opposite is true as well. It's those things that make us feel like we're better than others that actually produce nothing significant at all. It seems, with Him, small is big, and big is small. The cheers of the crowds don't mean much. The simple conversation where we helped someone means everything. Hundreds or thousands of people following us on social media isn't the big influence we think it is. Being kind and gracious to that gal who works at the grocery store does more than we know. A donation given with a pure and generous heart is a massive gift for the Kingdom. A million dollars given with a hidden agenda and a desire for recognition is a tiny gift for the Kingdom.

The Bible is full of God's upside-down principles:

The world tells us to exalt ourselves and climb the ladder of success.
God says to humble yourself so that He can be the one to lift you up. (1 Peter 5:6)

The world pushes us to live in division with those different from us.
God says to "love your enemies and pray for those who persecute you" *(Matthew 5:44).*

The world yells, "Live your best life now!"
God says this life is fading, and your best life is the one yet to come. (James 4:14; 1 Peter 1:3-5)

The world tells us how to fit in.
God empowers us to be set apart as difference-makers. (Matthew 5:13-16)

The world says death is the end of the story.
God used the death of Jesus to bring forth life, and He promises death will never again have the final word. (Romans 6:9-11)

01 | How does this stir your heart and help you consider a different perspective with something you're facing right now?

There are so many other examples of this upside-down pattern in Scripture, but one we will look at today is the pattern of less-than and greater-than. There is a consistent thread throughout the story of Scripture where God uses people society would view as less-than, and He proves to the world, through them, He is in fact greater-than.

We see this pattern most significantly with people who were considered less-than because of a situation they were walking through or a status they lacked:

Jacob was considered less-than because he was the youngest son, born without the privileges of the birthright that come with being the oldest brother.

Moses felt less-than because of his trouble with public speaking.

Women like Sarah and Hannah were thought of as less-than because they struggled with barrenness.

Gideon and King Saul were considered weaker and less significant because of their hometowns.

David was considered less-than because he was the youngest son and was left to tend the flocks while his older brothers were presented as the potential future kings of Israel.

Prophets of the Old Testament like Elijah, Elisha, Amos, Habakkuk and so many others were tasked with the responsibility of giving God's Word to God's people, only to be rejected and shunned. They must have felt less-than in those moments.

02 Have you ever felt less-than because of a situation or status in your own life or family? How has this affected you?

During Week 2, we looked at the book of Micah. Let's take another look at Micah 5:2 again today to notice something else from these scriptures talking about Bethlehem:

*"But you, O **Bethlehem** Ephrathah,*
*who are too **little** to be among the clans of Judah,*
from you shall come forth for me
one who is to be ruler in Israel,
whose coming forth is from of old,
from ancient days" (emphasis added).

The Hebrew word used to describe Bethlehem as *"little"* is *ṣāʿîr.* It can mean small, younger or insignificant.[38] In fact, this is the same word used to describe the younger sibling in a family, or one's social status within the family. (Genesis 19:31; Genesis 29:26; Joshua 9:26)[39]

We may be tempted to overlook some of our less-than moments because culture values the opposite, like success and superiority. That's when it's important for us to remember how Jesus came.

He came from this little, insignificant town called Bethlehem. (Matthew 2:1; Micah 5:2)

- Jesus was born in the shadow of scandal, to a mother who conceived before marriage. (Luke 2:4-6)
- Jesus was born into a lineage with some unexpected ancestors, including an adulterer and a prostitute. (Matthew 1:1-16)
- Jesus was raised in Nazareth. (John 1:46)
- Jesus was likely ordinary-looking. (Isaiah 53:2)
- Jesus chose fishermen and tax collectors as His disciples. (Matthew 4:18-22)
- Jesus ate and hung out with the social outcasts of the time, like:
  - A leper. (Luke 5:12-16)
  - A paralytic. (Luke 5:17-26)
  - A tax collector. (Luke 5:27-32)
  - A woman who was caught up in sin, and men caught up in hypocrisy.[40] (John 8:1-11)
  - A person afflicted with spiritual (demonic) torment. (Luke 8:26-39)

By the world's standard today, and even the times Jesus lived in, He was considered less- than, lowly and therefore unlikely to be the long-awaited Son of God. His own people, the Jews, doubted He was actually the Messiah!

03 | Go to Mark 6:3. What does it say about people's response to who Jesus was?

Why would God choose to reveal His greater-than power through these less-than realities and circumstances both in the life of people in the Old Testament and in the life of Jesus? There are a few reasons to consider:

Read 1 Corinthians 1:26-31.

- **This greater-than/less-than pattern reminds us there is nothing outside of God's capability.**

Read Ephesians 2:11-13.

- **This pattern reveals to us that no one who places their trust in Christ is disqualified in the Kingdom of God.**

Read Matthew 13:31-32.

- **This pattern challenges us to look for Jesus in seemingly small or insignificant ways.**

04 | What connections do you see in all of these scriptures within the pattern of less-than and greater-than?

God is in the business of bringing great things to life from less-than situations. Miraculous things from the mundane. Powerful things from what looks like weakness. Redeemed things from what seemed like nothing but a loss. God sending Jesus in the circumstances and way He did is only one example of pure evidence of this.

And for us, what if the next big step God wants us to take actually appears small by the world's standards? What if His great next step for us looks a little like less-than?

Loving our next-door neighbor who lives alone ...
Spending extra time with our child when we're exhausted ...
Going the extra mile for someone who can't repay us ...
Choosing to obediently stay in a place that isn't looking like how we thought it would ...
Giving our all in something we want to quit ...

Sometimes God is inviting us to be a part of great things He is doing all around us, but we may miss the invitation because of its appearance of smallness or insignificance. But we'll never know what that next step is if we don't *"listen for GOD's voice in everything [we] do, everywhere [we] go,"* as Proverbs 3:6 (MSG) instructs us. Each day we can look for His invitation to leave our plans behind to join Him in His wondrous work through small steps of obedience.

05 | To close today, pray about what your small step of obedience may be. How do the less-than moments and attributes of Jesus' life challenge you?

THE PATTERN OF CHAOS AND ORDER

Every circle of friends has "the party-planning friend."

They're usually the friend who keeps everyone together, who always has the details straight for celebrations, trips and more. Maybe they're a little type-A, but they provide structure and follow through on plans to keep things in order. Some of their friends operate just fine with chaos, but not them. And in the end, everyone around them benefits from their intentionality.

Interestingly enough, there's a pattern in Scripture that looks a lot like this: the pattern of chaos and order. Even though chaos is present in different stories of Scripture, it should bring a little bit of relief and reassurance that the Bible includes these very relatable stories. But even through these times of chaos, God consistently brings order to disordered situations. His faithfulness continues to bring unity even through the chaos sin causes. We can trace this pattern all the way to Jesus.

This is the *final pattern* we will look at this week, and it's actually the *first pattern* we see in Scripture. On Day 13, we talked about the creation story including a "void," but we will look at it from a different perspective today.

01 | Read Genesis 1:1-2. What kind of words are used to describe the state of the world at this point in creation?

— A NOTE FROM JOEL

The word "separated" here is the Hebrew word בָּדַל (bā·ḏǎl), which means division.

All of these descriptions are indicators of chaos. You see, Old Testament authors would have written from a particular historical and cultural context because of where they lived in the Ancient Near East. Topics like darkness and the sea were consistent images of chaos, disorder, disunity and destruction.

However, we know God doesn't leave the world in its original state. In the middle of chaos, God brings order through creation. And interestingly enough, He does so by separating or dividing.

02 | Read Genesis 1:1-18 and underline every time you see the word *"separated."*

God separates the light from the darkness.
God separates the waters, creating heaven.
God separates the water into one place and creates earth/dry land, or earth and seas.
God separates the lights/sun and stars.
God separates sea creatures from air creatures.

In each act of division God institutes divine order. But because of the events following Genesis 1, rebellion interrupts divine order and there is a division God never intended among people. This separation, a form of chaos, plays out in two ways:

- Separation between God and man (sin).
- Separation among men (conflict).

All of us have experienced the chaos of *conflict*. The situations may be different, and the degree of intensity will vary, but if you do life with people, you will have conflict. It's just part of being a human on this side of eternity.

Even though conflict is common, that doesn't make it any easier. And this evidence of conflict can be traced all the way back to the first family of creation.

03 | Read Genesis 4:1-8. What was the result of this conflict?

Adam and Eve's descendants continued to populate the earth. And the same command God gave to Adam and Eve in the Garden in Genesis 1:28, to *"be fruitful and multiply and fill the earth and subdue it,"* was given to their descendants. But they would not carry out this command as God intended. Over and over the people rebelled.

04 | Look at Genesis 11 to read about what took place in the plains of Shinar where the people gathered. Instead of being a reflection of the goodness and glory of God, what did the people do?

It's important to note that plains don't have mountains, which is where people believed God met with humanity during this time.[41] So their rebellion continued and resulted in the building of the Tower of Babel. Besides attempting to make a name for themselves, this tower was their solution for God to come down and meet with them, but it was really nothing more than a manufactured mountain built out of idolatry.[42]

Let's take a closer look at some of the events that followed:
Lysa here. Remember, anything we turn to instead of God to satisfy us or to save us is an idol. It's a false god.

CHAOS	The Tower of Babel is a form of rebellion in the plains of Shinar. This rebellion results in the division of humanity by diversifying tongues (languages). (Genesis 11:1-9)
CHAOS	As a result of this punishment, the nations spread out into the world, including the Philistines, Hittites, Egyptians, etc., and are in constant war against God's people of Israel.
ORDER	Different judges like Gideon, Samson, Jephthah, etc. are able to establish temporary order in the midst of the division.
ORDER	The united kingdom is established under Saul and David.
CHAOS	Because of the nations that David conquers, he has blood on his hands and cannot build the temple.
ORDER	Solomon builds the temple.
CHAOS	Solomon's reign of peace ends in household rebellion and the division of the kingdom into the Northern and Southern tribes.

Throughout this pattern of chaos and order, we see a few things taking place. In the presence of chaos in Genesis 1, God creates something from nothing, and His creation is good. His good creation rebels, which ends in people warring against each other and ultimately against God. The people choose sin, which brings chaos into God's order. This requires a holy and just God to execute punishment. But God's mercy and kindness is always present, even in, and arguably especially in, the midst of punishment. The punishment from God isn't an act of cruelty to the people. His discipline has a purpose — to bring back eventual order.

God's goal is to establish order: order between man and God (reconciliation) and order among men (peace, unity). What is the evidence of this? Jesus. This is where we see the redemption of Jesus revealed all through the Bible. Jesus redemptively reverses the division of humanity through His work on the cross. In Acts 10:36 we read, *"You know the message God sent to the people of Israel, announcing the good news of peace through Jesus Christ, who is Lord of all"* (NIV). This means what was preached to the Israelites is now available to the gentiles. Acts 10:35 is a key verse because it says *"in every nation,"* so it sets a global, multi-ethnic, international context for this beautiful redemptive reversal.

Even though judges and kings temporarily established order, it didn't fix the spiritual separation between God and man. But God continued His faithfulness to institute divine order by sending Jesus, the only One who could provide lasting order.

05 | Read Isaiah 4:2-6, Isaiah 11:1-9 and Isaiah 55:3-4. Take note of some of these prophecies about Jesus through the lens of chaos and order.

We will continue to experience chaos in our lives today. That is the evidence of our sin-soaked world. However, there are two truths we want to leave you with today to provide perspective in spite of this:

- Jesus closed the separation, caused by sin, between God and humanity by making a relationship with God possible for anyone who places their trust in Him. (John 1:12-13; John 14:6; Titus 2:11-14)
- The Holy Spirit empowers us to move beyond chaos in our world and earthly relationships to pursue order in the form of peace and unity. (Acts 1:8; Ephesians 3:16) Through this, we are actually invited to participate in the pattern. We may not be able to avoid conflict, but we can pray about what Jesus would have us do in the middle of it.

06 | When you think about the word "order," what words come to mind? How might you be able to participate in peace and unity in your own life today?

To close today, meditate on the words of Paul from Colossians 1:19-23:

*"For in him all the **fullness** of God was pleased to **dwell,** and through him to **reconcile** to himself all things, whether on earth or in heaven, **making peace** by the blood of his cross. And you, who once were alienated and hostile in mind, doing evil deeds, he has now **reconciled** in his body of flesh by his death, in order to present you holy and blameless and above reproach before him, if indeed you **continue in the faith, stable and steadfast, not shifting from the hope of the gospel that you heard,** which has been proclaimed in all creation under heaven, and of which I, Paul, became a minister"* (emphasis added).

Now, let's pray together and prepare our hearts for Week 4. *God, thank You for continuing to reveal Yourself to me through Scripture. Through everything I continue to study, I pray I would see more of Jesus and it would drive me into an even deeper relationship with Him. I thank You today for Your everlasting faithfulness. I trust You through every situation I am facing right now. In Jesus' Name, Amen.*

WEEK
four

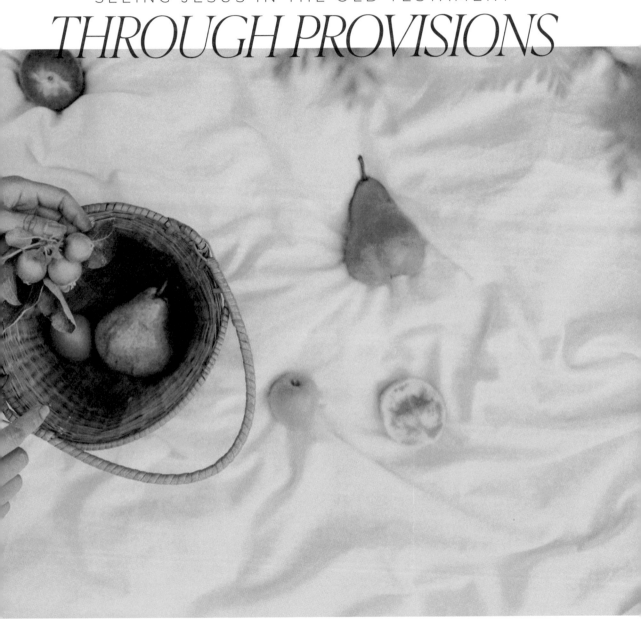

THROUGH PROVISIONS

INTRODUCTION TO PROVISIONS

Lysa here. Can I share something before we get into this week's study? Over the last several years, I've spent night after night lifting up gut-honest prayers to the Lord over things in my life that I can't control, change or provide a different outcome for. So many times I've woken up in the middle of the night feeling overwhelmed by everything I am facing. When I feel like the weight of overwhelming heartbreak is on me at 2 a.m. and I feel utterly alone, my prayers get reduced to tear-filled cries. Often, all I can pray is, "Jesus, I love You, and You love me. Please help me."

I know what it feels like to pray so many prayers begging for God's mighty intervention, but after an extended period of time with no change, we can feel unheard, alone and neglected.

When we're in this place, our hearts ache. Our minds race. We might not admit this in Bible study or with our friends. But in quiet moments, alone, we secretly wonder: Where has Jesus gone?

We've been there, too. We've made countless suggestions, desperate for God to do something. When we fix our eyes on those anticipated outcomes, we can sometimes miss how and when God *is* answering our prayers.

We see this pattern of people missing the evidence of God's care and provision throughout Scripture and, ironically, even in the story of Jesus' life. He was the answer to Israel's long-lifted-up prayers for a Messiah, but so many missed God's faithful reply because Jesus didn't show up like they expected. Jesus wasn't an earthly king who came to give temporary victory over the oppressive Roman government, like the people at the time begged God for. He came to bring everlasting victory by becoming the eternal King who died on a cross to save His people. And Jesus wasn't a king born into a palace. No, our savior had much humbler beginnings.

Luke 2:4 sets the scene for the arrival of Jesus: *"So Joseph also went up from the town of Nazareth in Galilee to Judea, to Bethlehem the town of David, because he belonged to the house and line of David"* (NIV).

From the very start, Jesus' birth in Bethlehem fulfilled God's promise for a Messiah. (Micah 5:2) Even the very name of this tiny town — "house of bread" — is a prophetic declaration of future provision. Please don't miss the significance here: The house of bread was where the Bread of Life was born. (John 6:35) Bread is also mentioned in part of the Lord's Prayer in Matthew 6 where Jesus teaches us to pray for *"daily bread"* (v. 11). Jesus would also then go on and model that man does not live by bread alone but by the Word of God.

You see, God's promise of provision through Jesus is available to us today. Even when we feel abandoned as we wait for answered prayers, Jesus is our Daily Bread. His very birth was marked by provision and He has been our physical and spiritual provision from the very beginning of time. We even see a pointing to the salvation of Jesus in Genesis 3. God provided animal skins for Adam and Eve to cover themselves after they sinned and realized they were naked. On that day, it was the blood of a sacrificial animal that was shed to provide a covering. On the cross, Jesus provided the ultimate covering of our sins by giving His own life.

As we study how God provided for His people throughout the Old Testament, all the way to the provision of Jesus Himself coming to earth, we have an opportunity to remember that God always keeps His promises. And when we remember this, that same reassurance will ground us today in our seemingly unanswered prayers and empty places where we're wanting assurance of God's intervention and provision.

After all, Jesus is the best promise kept of all. Our most complete provision and portion. (Psalm 73:26) Our forever reminder that we are not left lost, wandering or helpless. He is the only lasting, satisfying nourishment and perfect sustenance for every longing in our souls.

Let's dig into Week 4, friend.

PROVISION REVEALED IN PRIESTS

As a result of the fall in Genesis 3, there's a progressive feeling in the Old Testament that God grows distant from His people. We go from reading about God walking, talking and intimately communing with Adam and Eve in the Garden to what feels like a complete silence and absence of His presence in the exilic and postexilic periods of Israelite history. That kind of progressive distance from God can feel confusing and maybe even add to our anxiety about Him. *Will He be there for us?*

It would be like if you went from doing life with a friend every single day to a long-distance friendship because they moved across the country. You used to talk every day about the smallest details of your day, but now you struggle to catch up even about the big moments. The physical separation creates an uncomfortable and unfamiliar absence that, over time, becomes an unfortunate new normal.

Even if you've never had to try making a long-distance friendship work, you can probably relate to feeling disconnected (emotionally, spiritually, conversationally, etc.) from people in your life or maybe even God.

01 | Describe a time when you felt like God was distant or silent. What do you say internally in these moments or even seasons?

This week is all about uncovering Old Testament examples of how God continually provided for His people, and how those provisions can help us see the ultimate provision of God sending Jesus, who in His humanity had real skin, real emotions and even experienced hunger and thirst. Jesus endured all of our human needs. God knew we needed atonement for our sins and that only Jesus could provide that atonement. But He also knew we would need a living, breathing example of how to live in a sin-soaked world and still follow God, love people and not fall into the traps of the enemy. Jesus would be perfect in divinity and at the same time made fully human in every way. (Hebrews 2:17)

Why is this important for us to know? God heard the cries of the people all through the Old Testament and knew His provision of Jesus would be the answer. More rules placed on the people would never save them from their sin. Only Jesus could do that. And when Jesus came, He would feel what we feel. Suffer like we suffer. Get rejected by others like we get rejected. Jesus was sinless. But He knew the sting of being sinned against.

Friend, when we start to feel God is absent, like the children of Israel must have felt many times, we must know He always has a bigger plan in the works ... for even better provision than we know to ask for.

Today's study actually starts with an unexpected discovery. Even when it appeared God was absent, He was working out provision for His people in ways that would best serve them. But it wouldn't always look like what they thought or even what they hoped for.

You see, as sin continued its evil effects on people, God established a system that would include three positions to help care for His people: priests, prophets and kings. These formal positions were not just necessary but actually essential to fill the gap of separation, created by sin, between man and God. We're going to spend the next three days diving into each of these categories, starting today with priests.

Priests were not uncommon in the Ancient Near East, and each priest functioned primarily as an "intercessor" between God and humanity.[43]

02 | What comes to mind when you hear the word "intercessor"?

We first see priests appear in Exodus 19:5-6. Let's go there together:

*"'Now therefore, if you will indeed obey my voice and keep my covenant, you shall be my treasured possession among all peoples, for all the earth is mine; and you shall be to me a kingdom of **priests** and a holy nation.' These are the words that you shall speak to the people of Israel."* (emphasis added)

In a striking statement, God says that all of Israel would function as "priests" — a holy people separate from the people of the world — to identify themselves as the people of God. This is an important thought, as we think about the New Testament and how the Church functions today.

First Peter 2:9 says, *"But you are a chosen race, a royal priesthood, a holy nation, a people for his own possession, that you may proclaim the excellencies of him who called you out of darkness into his marvelous light."* This idea is important because it's another example of the connection between the Old and New Testaments. There is a progression from what God proclaimed to the people of Israel (in the Old Testament) to the fulfillment of the New Testament Church being made up of all people being priests. We no longer need priests to be our mediators. Because of Jesus we all have direct access to communicate with God.

Now, reread Exodus 19:5-6. In order for the people of God to live up to the standard of a "priestly nation," they needed leadership, guidance and help. This is why God established the Levitical priesthood from the line of Aaron to teach the people how to be a kingdom of priests. In other words, a nation set apart for God, to point everyone else to God.

Why does this matter to us? This is the role of the modern-day Church. We are supposed to be set apart for God, to point everyone outside of the Church to God.

03 | What are some of the ways you've chosen to set yourself apart for the purpose of pointing others to God? Think about your actions, words, attitudes, habits, etc.

Lysa here. When I hear the words "set apart," I wonder: How do we practically do this on a daily basis? I want to be faithful to this while being authentically me. I don't want to be a performer of fake holiness. Nor do I want to develop a holier-than-thou attitude. So one of my favorite ways to pursue being set apart is by connecting God's Word to my everyday life. I love to read Bible verses in the morning and then intentionally look for the application of some part of those verses in a situation I face that day. I don't want to just read the Scriptures for information or inspiration. I want to make it my daily practice of learning to be "set apart" that day through application of the Scripture verses I read. Then I will be more equipped to change my attitude, action, reaction, thoughts, words to others, and perspectives.

Those daily applications will aid in my transformation. The more intentional I am with getting into God's Word and God's Word getting into me, the more clearly I will sense the Holy Spirit leading, guiding and redirecting me towards things that honor God. The Holy Spirit is the gift that Jesus gave us to help comfort, convict, challenge, encourage and direct us in our daily lives. We won't do this perfectly, but that doesn't mean we don't try at all.

As God's people we, like the children of Israel, are called to be set apart and God equips us to live this out.

In the Old Testament the priests of God were anointed by oil as a public declaration of being set apart. (Exodus 29) In the New Testament and even now, the people of God are anointed with the Holy Spirit who abides in them. The presence of the Spirit in us is the sign and symbol that marks us as priests. This is significant for us to remember.

04 | How does understanding this encourage and empower you?

Historically, there are three duties priests performed:

- Represent the people before God.
- Perform sacrifices.
- Provide counsel and structure.

The work of the priests in the Old Testament took place primarily in the temple. It's important to point out that the temple was the place where the presence of God resided, most specifically in the Holy of Holies. The temple was also the location where sacrifice would take place to make atonement for the sin of the people of God. The priests were responsible not just for performing these sacrifices but also for the overall care and upkeep of the temple.

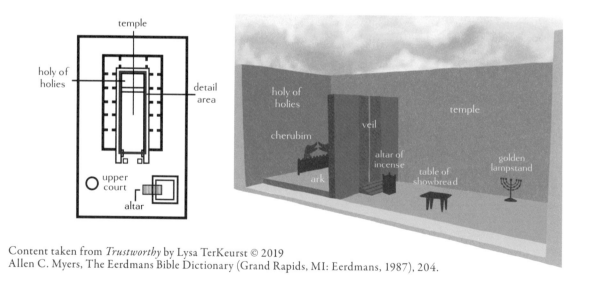

Content taken from *Trustworthy* by Lysa TerKeurst © 2019
Allen C. Myers, The Eerdmans Bible Dictionary (Grand Rapids, MI: Eerdmans, 1987), 204.

However, it was only the *high priest* who once a year would enter into the Holy of Holies to make a sacrifice for the sin of the people on the "Day of Atonement." (Leviticus 16:4)[44] The high priest was also held to a higher standard, and any sin that the high priest committed brought guilt upon the entire nation and resulted in the need for a special sacrifice. (Leviticus 4:1-12)

In addition to being an intercessor, God provided earthly priests so His people would be led and instructed in holy living as the people of God, as God is holy. But because these human priests were still mortal, sinful and imperfect, their actions disgraced the temple. The priests had to repeatedly offer sacrifices not only on behalf of the people of God but for their own sins as well.

— A NOTE FROM JOEL

The Day of Atonement took place on the 10th day of the seventh month where the Israelites would fast and deal with sin through sacrifice at the temple.

These Old Testament priests did provide temporary access and intercession for the people of God, but they also revealed a large hole that no one mortal, sinful and imperfect could ever fill. The people of God still needed someone who could accomplish the role of a priest in completeness, which is exactly who Jesus is.

05 | Read Hebrews 2:14-18. What does verse 17 refer to Jesus as?

God provided a way for His people to have a connection to Him through the priests of the Old Testament. But even as these priests stood in the gap of separation and assisted in sacrifice, it would never be enough. While they were still God's faithful provision, Jesus embodies what these Old Testament priests could never be: a High Priest without sin, yet completely able to empathize with the temptation of sin. In his book *Gentle and Lowly,* Dane Ortlund discusses not just what Jesus Christ has done but who Jesus is and His deepest heart for His people. Ortlund says it this way: "The various high priests through Israel's history were sinfully weak; Jesus the High Priest was sinlessly weak."[45]

Simply put, Ortlund says Jesus "is the High Priest to end all high priests."[46]

06 Read Hebrews 4:14-16. Even though Jesus' sinlessness could make Him seem unapproachable toww us, what do these verses instruct us to do anyway?

The blood of the sin offerings the priests made in the temple covered the sins from the community of people on the Day of Atonement, but as our High Priest, Jesus Himself was and is the sacrifice that made this possible and removes our sins through His own blood.

Instead of needing an external sacrifice, Jesus Himself was the sacrifice. He who knew no sin took on the sins of the world. (2 Corinthians 5:21) The road to the cross He bore paved the way for a path of righteousness for us.

07 Look at Hebrews 5:1-4. What stands out to you?

Remember the distinctives of what the Old Testament priests were to do? Represent the people before God, perform sacrifices, and provide counsel and structure. Let's look at how these things manifest in Jesus Himself:

1. **Jesus is the ultimate representative for humanity before God and intercedes for us.** (See Romans 8:34; Hebrews 7:25.)

2. **Jesus Himself was the Sacrificial Lamb, who made atonement in finality through the shedding of His own blood.** (See John 1:29; 1 John 2:2; Hebrews 1:3.)

3. **Jesus provides counsel and direction to us through the Holy Spirit,** (John 14:26) **who is the Spirit of Christ.** (See Philippians 1:19; Acts 16:7; Galatians 4:6.)

Let's close today by pausing to reflect on this truth: Because of Jesus, even when God feels absent, we still have full access to Him. This provision of direct access should forever remind us that we are not insignificant. We are not just another face in the crowd to God. He wants us close because of His love of us, His intimate connection with us and His important assignments for us.

What a gift.

PROVISION REVEALED IN PROPHETS

This is Lysa and I just want to do a tender check-in with you. Have you ever prayed or cried out to God, asking Him to give you a picture of the future so you don't feel so shaken by today? I have. On the one hand, I know God is in control and He can take everything and somehow work things together for good. But on the other hand, what if the good He is working out isn't what we would agree to as good?

Eventual good still doesn't ease the ache and heartbreak of today.

Eventual good can feel so far away that you wonder if it really will ever happen.

Eventual good doesn't make the panic of this moment less intense.

Eventual good can seem like throwing a penny in a fountain — like nothing more than a thinly whispered wish.

But what if all of our uncertainty is because we haven't understood that Jesus is our prophet who daily assures us with certainty in the midst of uncertainty? And who daily guides us through hard circumstances and never abandons us?

While I know Jesus knows the future, I haven't often thought of how this can help assure me today. But think about it. Jesus leads us today with a confident knowing of exactly how all of our tomorrows will play out. He knows how to get us through everything we are facing like a guide who knows the path and how to avoid treacherous terrain. He knows how we are feeling as humans with real fears, real heartbreak, real sorrow, real anxiety and real effects of sin. He knows what we should do and shouldn't do. He knows where we need to go. He knows how to get from where we are today to the promised good God has in store.

I don't often think of Jesus as a prophet. And I'm not sure I've ever thought that His role as a prophet could be particularly comforting to me. That's why today's study is surprisingly important for us. Remember, if we can see Jesus in unexpected ways in the Old Testament, we are more likely to believe He's working in the unseen places of our lives today.

So what was the role of the prophets in the Old Testament? And who are some of the prophets who point us to seeing Jesus as a prophet as well?

A prophet served as a mouthpiece and guide to the people of God. A prophet was God's gracious provision of assurance so the people of God didn't feel alone and so they wouldn't panic in the midst of unexpected circumstances. The prophets received a message from God and delivered this message to the people of God. This is known as *prophecy*.

01 | What can you recall from Week 2 when we studied prophecy? Jot down a few thoughts.

When you think about prophecy, perhaps a mystical image comes to mind, like a person with a crystal ball foretelling the future. But in Scripture, prophets were individuals who communicated divine messages from God to the people of God. They spoke truth about present situations and identified the outcomes of punishment for evil or reward for righteous behavior. They were both men (*nābî'*) and women (*nĕbî'â*), prophets and prophetesses, who were literally "called of God" and spoke as representatives of God.

And while we spent Week 2 looking at Old Testament prophecies that foretold the coming of Jesus, today we're going to dive deeper into how He specifically and personally guides us, and through His guidance we can be filled with assurance and confidence.

In order to do this we're going to look at the role of prophets in the Old Testament so we can see how God provided guidance and assurance to the people of that day, which can help us see what Jesus does for us today.

Sometimes, we can make the mistake of thinking God isn't providing for us when the answers to our cries and prayers don't look like we thought. We want our needs met right away and in our way. We want God to be clear with His assurances, too. I've often wished God would appear in my room in such a way that we could have a face-to-face conversation. Or at least that He would write me a letter with clear instructions and tender assurances that everything is under control and will be OK.

But what if I told you the longing for direct communication from God is not unique to us? People have always had this longing. So let's find the first glimpse of how God answered this longing through prophets in the Old Testament. Today, we're going to study the Old Testament prophet Elijah and then see how Elijah's life compares and contrasts to the greater prophet, Jesus.

Elijah was a prophet of God. (1 Kings 18:36) Sometimes the Bible uses different words to describe the same thing. Another phrase we see in the Old Testament used as a synonym for prophet is "man of God" (*'îš hā'ĕlōhîm*). "Man of God" identifies a person who is commissioned by God with a divine message to communicate to humanity (sometimes to the people of God, sometimes to foreign nations). This phrase was used to describe Elijah.

We can best understand the role of the prophet as that of a "mouthpiece" or a trumpet. Today, we may think of this like a microphone. While a microphone that is plugged into speakers can broadcast a message to a vast audience, the microphone is useless without the voice and breath of the person speaking into it.

This is what is happening with the prophets of the Old Testament, including Elijah. God is the voice and breath, the origin and source of the message, and His microphone is the prophets.

God sends Elijah to the people of Israel as a provision to instruct and guide them. God's message proclaimed through Elijah was for the people to turn away from the false god Baal and back to the one true God, Yahweh. In an epic showdown (1 Kings 18) Elijah issued a challenge between his God (Yahweh) and the false god of Ahab and Jezebel (Baal). The outcome was Yahweh showing His might and burning up the altar, and the subsequent deaths of the false prophets of Baal. (1 Kings 18:40) Needless to say, Jezebel was not happy that her prophets were killed and that her god looked utterly helpless (because he was).

A NOTE FROM LYSA

Remember what we learned in Week 1 ... "Yahweh" is the intimate name of God given to the Israelites; it was a name that reminded the people of the greatness of God and that they were His possession and inheritance.

Before we get too far, let's make a connection between the prophet Elijah and how he is a glimpse of Jesus. God sent Jesus, His own Son, to guide the world out of the darkness and deceit of evil powers (false gods) and back into the family of the one true God. What the prophet Elijah does in this one incident of defeating evil, Jesus will accomplish in the ultimate defeat of evil for eternity.

Prophets were a great provision given to the people of God, but they also point to the greater provision of Jesus. While prophets like Elijah were seen as mouthpieces, Jesus as a prophet is not simply just the mouthpiece of God; He is God incarnate and therefore the very voice of God Himself.

— A NOTE FROM LYSA

When you read "Jesus is God incarnate" this means God takes on human flesh. This does not mean He ceases to exist as God. This just means He now truly, in every way, can relate to humanity. If you've ever been confused about how it is possible for God to still be God and at the same time take on the form of Jesus, remember this: God is one in essence and distinct in the personhood of Father, Son and Holy Spirit. I once heard someone explain the Trinity using ice, water and steam. At first this makes sense because ultimately it is all water but presented in various forms. However, this is where this example falls apart. The water can't be ice at the same time as being steam. God is Father, Son and Holy Spirit all at the same time. One in essence yet distinct in persons. This means He didn't abandon being God when Jesus walked the earth as God the Son. There is never a moment in history when God the Father, God the Son and God the Spirit aren't all actively working together and in tandem to bring rescue and redemption to people by defeating evil.

Source: Michael Reeves, *Delighting in the Trinity: An Introduction to the Christian Faith* (Downers Grove, Ill: IVP Academic, 2012), pp. 34-35.

God spoke through Elijah, and God showed His power by sending fire from Heaven.

When Jesus speaks, God speaks. When Jesus came from heaven, He brought with Him the very power of heaven to earth. The greatness of Jesus as the better prophet can be found in what's called a "redemptive reversal" in Matthew 4:1-11. What a man like Elijah can only do in part and with human flaws, Jesus does in full with perfection.

A "redemptive reversal" can be defined as an image or description of a situation in the Bible that seems to be tragic but then, later in Scripture, is retold as a triumph. The tragic situation is reversed and redeemed and replaced with triumph.

Take a look at the chart below:

Elijah (1 Kings 19)	Jesus (Matthew 4:1-11; Luke 4:1-12)
Elijah is led into the wilderness because of fear. (1 Kings 19:3)	Jesus is led into the wilderness by the Spirit. (Matthew 4:1)
Elijah looks for a way out of his plight. (1 Kings 19:4)	Jesus looks to God and is obedient in His plight. (Matthew 4:1)
Elijah is fed and taken care of by an *angel of the LORD* in the middle of his hunger and thirst (1 Kings 19:5-7).	Jesus endures hunger in the wilderness. (Matthew 4:2-4)
The food Elijah eats sustains him throughout his 40-day journey because *"the journey is too great"* for him (1 Kings 19:7-8).	Jesus endures 40 days of fasting and is tempted by the devil. The journey is not too great for Jesus, and after He is found faithful, the angels minister to Him. (Matthew 4:11)

And where did all of this provision take place? For both Elijah and Jesus, the provision occurred in the wilderness of the desert. Anytime we read about the people of God being in the desert or the wilderness, we can know this is the equivalent of some of the hard and challenging things we will go through as well. In desert times, we often must face our inability to fix things on our own. We all must face the reality that we need the provision of God.

And we must learn that, even in the face of adversity, we can trust God. We may fear not being able to control the timing. We may fear things not going the way we want. We may fear that God will abandon us. But it is in this unexpected place, where God continually shows up to provide and care for His children, that we develop more and more trust. What Jesus endured shows us once again that He knows how to stay steadfast in His obedience in the midst of human suffering and uncertainty. Jesus is the greater prophet and our ultimate provision as advocate and intercessor to God on our behalf.

02 | As you consider your own wilderness times, either of suffering or testing, how did you see God provide for you?

God gave the people of Israel a prophet in Elijah as a form of provision to guide them and fill them with assurance, and to remind them of the one true God of the heavens and the earth. But remember, Elijah was an imperfect prophet, not the perfect prophet. God sent the greatest provision in Jesus. He (and only He) is the ultimate prophet and the embodiment of confident assurance to us.

PROVISION REVEALED IN KINGS

Hi friend ... *Lysa here*. You see, you and I have a lot in common. But I would imagine one of the most shared longings we all have is the desire to feel safe.

In my early 20s, I had some friends who had the most beautiful golden retriever dog. Everyone around him fell in love with him. His cuteness made even his rowdiness fun and adorable. The one big issue with him was his absolute terror of thunder and fireworks. He couldn't get his bearings when one of these loud sounds rumbled or popped anywhere near him. He would run in circles, whining, and then tear through the house looking for somewhere to hide. He would barrel through a room and knock over anything in his way to get to a spot that made him feel more covered and hidden.

Well, one Fourth of July, the family left early in the morning to go to a parade and then to a cookout. They hadn't planned on staying for their friend's fireworks show but time got away from them and they didn't get home until much later than planned. They had assumed their dog would be just fine since they put him in the bathroom with food, water, toys and music to camouflage any firework noises.

What they hadn't thought about was him jumping into the tub with such force he turned the tub faucet on. He was big enough and tall enough to still be able to stand in the tub while the water filled it up. So he was never in danger. But the house didn't fare so well. The tub overflowed and completely flooded their house. When they pulled into the driveway that night, they instantly knew something was wrong. Water was pouring from underneath their garage doors.

Their dog, of course, had no thoughts of flooding their house. He was simply desperate because of his fear to get into that tub and feel more safe.

When we FEEL UNSAFE it can lead us TO PURSUE *anything* we perceive will PROVIDE SAFETY.

I'll raise my hand here and readily admit I have this struggle. When something happens and suddenly fear grips me with intensity, I can say things I wouldn't normally say. Or I can jump to worst-case scenarios and let my panic drive me to make decisions I wouldn't normally make.

Out of desperation, I can betray my best intentions. I want to trust God, but my fear drives me to want that threatening feeling to go away more.

01 | How do you personally relate to this? When has fear driven you to say or do things you wouldn't otherwise have said and done?

Sometimes the intentions we have are good, but the timing and motivation behind those intentions and desires can turn good things into reckless things. Now that we've studied priests and prophets, let's look at the third example of God's provision: kings. As we learned in Week 1 when studying David, Israel had God as their king. But the Israelites got impatient because all the other nations around them had impressive kings ... or so they thought. They feared if they didn't have the presence of an earthly king, they would be vulnerable to attack. They went against God's plan and His warnings of the dangers of an earthly king. Their fear of their enemies was greater than their trust in God.

Today, we will see how the request for a king by God's people may not have been motivated by wrong intentions. It's absolutely normal to want to ensure our safety (see Genesis 17:6,16 and Deuteronomy 17:14-15). And it can feel extremely dysregulating when we feel unsafe. But I often have to remind myself something about feelings. **Feelings should be indicators, not dictators.** In other words, feelings should make us aware that something needs to be addressed, but feelings shouldn't dictate how we act and react. In today's study we will discover how important it is for us to continually remind ourselves of this.

When it comes to safety, the Israelites were actually in the safest spot because they were led by God, who had supreme power, wisdom and perfect intentions for the good of His people. They looked to God for all their needs and He was faithful to care for them as their Divine King. The biblical term for this idea is that Israel was ruled by a "theocracy."[47]

A NOTE FROM JOEL

This word for "theocracy" comes from the Greek "θεός/theos," which means "God" and can be literally translated as "God rule." The Jewish historian Josephus first used this word to describe the Israelites as being under the direct rule and reign of God.

Where the Israelites got into trouble is when they looked at the other countries and believed they were better cared for by the presence of an earthly king than the presence of their God, who they couldn't physically see. So, instead of trusting God, who had always demonstrated Himself faithful to them, they let their feelings run rampant and dictate their actions of distrust. This is why it is so important for us to remember, even when we can't physically see God or even understand what He's doing, that His character has always been to provide for His people. This is what the Israelites forgot.

02 | What are some areas of your life right now where you feel more led by your feelings of fear rather than the assurance of God's protection, provision and presence?

As we've studied provisions this week, we also must remember that God's provision is an overflow of who He always has been and who He is today. So what does this mean to you and me? Because God's character never changes, the assurance of Him providing for us will never change. And let's just mark this moment by declaring that this is true even in the dark places of fear, hurt and uncertainty. What the people of God didn't understand is that God was going to bring them not just an earthly king but the ultimate eternal King: Jesus. Their desire for a king wasn't bad. But they got motivated by fear to demand that God give them an earthly king in their timing rather than God's timing. "Motivation" and "timing" are two words we need to unpack.

But first let's once again acknowledge God hears, considers, interacts with and even responds to the pleas of His people. Let's use the framework of Israel asking for a king to teach us how to be more mindful of our motivations and why it's so important to trust in God's timing.

03 | Go to 1 Samuel 8:4-9. What's going on in the text here?

Let's unpack motivations and timing a little bit more.

Motivations	Timing
The elders of Israel are motivated to regain a sense of safety and security. Their fear drives them to want their solution of an earthly king more than trusting God.	Israel is in a unique moment in its history as a nation. Up until this time, the people have been led by God through direct rule and authority. God used prophets like Moses and judges like Joshua to communicate His divine decree and will to the people. As one Old Testament scholar says, "By requesting a human king, the people rupture Yahweh's exclusive attribution as king."[47] This is a good reminder that a good thing at the wrong time will be a bad thing. Timing matters, and trusting in the One who holds and directs time itself is always the safest place for us.

04 | Who is getting rejected by the people?

Samuel is the prophet speaking on behalf of God to the people at this time. Adding to the fear of the people is the fact that Samuel is about to die and none of his sons are qualified to take over the role of being the mouthpiece of God. So now the people are afraid that not only will they not have an earthly king, but they also won't have the connection to God through Samuel the prophet. In their desperation, they come up with their own solution.

05 | Let's look at 1 Samuel 8:5. What did the elders say about Samuel's sons? Where do the elders look for their "model" of kingship?

It's shocking when God acknowledges His people are not rejecting Samuel — they are rejecting Him! God is the perfect solution to their fear. Yet they reject the perfect solution because they prefer an immediate solution. They reject the warnings from God because they prefer the solution they thought up themselves.

06 | How does this challenge you personally right now?

07 | Read 1 Samuel 8:10-22. What stands out to you about Samuel's warning, given the context above?

The people of Israel failed to realize God was already the King they wanted and needed. He is the Righteous Judge and Divine Warrior leading them into battle and claiming victory — even eternal victory beyond just the physical battles at hand. Plus, God had plans for the future King Jesus, but of course His Kingship would be established in God's timing. The people subverted that timing and took matters into their own hands by asking and pleading for a king to meet their immediate needs because they let their fear override their trust of God. They didn't surrender the control of their own timing and desires. And in turn, they asked for a lesser version of what God had already provided and planned to provide through King Jesus.

— A NOTE FROM JOEL

Consider these scriptures as you process what we've been learning: Psalm 139:23-24, Psalm 51:10, 2 Corinthians 13:5 and 1 Corinthians 11:28.

08 | How does looking at this story in Scripture challenge you as you examine some of the ways you might control timing and seek to get your desires met in your own way? Remember, these don't always have to be bad desires ... They could be good desires being sought in wrong ways.

What the people looked for in their first king appeared good on the outside but turned out to be a disaster. After this first king, Saul, we find a king who more closely matches the kind of leader God desires: David.

09 | Read 2 Samuel 8:15. How is David's kingship described?

Let's take a look at these two words: *"justice"* and *"equity"* (also translated "righteousness" [v. 15]). When the terms "justice" (*miš·pāṭ*) and "equity" (*ṣā·ḏăq*) are used together in the Old Testament, they are attributed to the character of God. (Job 37:23; Psalm 33:5; Proverbs 8:20; Isaiah 5:16; Jeremiah 9:24; Micah 7:9)[49] This tells us God desired the kings of Israel to reflect His justice and righteousness. Many times, the prophets of the Old Testament were responding to a lack of justice or a perversion of righteousness, which is why it was important for a godly king to reflect the righteousness and justice of God.

So not only was the king supposed to judge, but he was also to be a king who would battle on behalf of the people. Again, we find David as a king who matches this ideal to a degree. David's royal life is filled with heroic military exploits and accolades starting with the defeat of Goliath and the victory over tens of thousands of Philistines. (1 Samuel 18:7-8; 1 Samuel 18:30; 1 Samuel 23:5; 2 Samuel 5:17-25) However, the narrator of 1 and 2 Samuel places a key phrase to coincide with David's victories.

10 | Read 1 Samuel 18:14, 2 Samuel 5:10 and 2 Samuel 8:6,14. What is the key idea and what does this tell us about David's victories?

In each of these examples, we are reminded that God was with David. In a sense, **what makes a king great is that king's nearness to the King of kings**. Human kingship came with serious flaws but also created a deep awareness of the longing for something better. For someone better. And as we will continue to discover throughout the duration of this study, this ideal King could only be fully accomplished in Jesus as the one true King.

How can we be sure of this? Because we see in the New Testament that Jesus is the long-awaited King. However, Jesus would execute justice and equity in a different way: the shedding of His own blood to make atonement for sin once and for all. Jesus would enter into a cosmic battle with sin and death on the cross and would defeat death and remove the sting of sin through death itself. While David's body lay in a royal tomb, Jesus' body rose and walked out of the tomb. Jesus is the eternal King of kings.

As we wrap up, take out your Bible and read Ephesians 1:18-21. As you consider the power Jesus displays as the King of kings, think about how this encourages you in the places of your heart that are struggling to feel safe. Today, we've seen how the kings of the Old Testament left things so unfulfilled. All that the elders of Israel longed for they still didn't experience in fullness. But in Jesus, as the King of kings, **we don't just have a King who rules sovereignly, but He's also there presently and personally.** He isn't a distant, untouchable ruler. He came down to us. When we read about the kings of the Old Testament, we can see a picture of Jesus being what the people of God were so desperate for all along.

PROVISION REVEALED IN MANNA

There's no desperation quite like the moment of realizing you're racing out the door, late for a meeting, and you hear your stomach growl.

Yep ... you totally forgot to eat breakfast. The frustration from the hurried pace of the morning, compounded within the pit of your stomach, leaves you feeling not just hungry but *hangry*. Hungry AND angry.

Lysa here. This is me.
Joel here. This is me ... worse.

The chaotic emotions we feel when we have physical needs demanding to be met leaves us feeling vulnerable and sometimes even desperate. While we may poke fun at our tendency to become "hangry" at times, these feelings of desperation from lack of physical supply are actually found in the Old Testament quite often.

You see, for over 400 years in Egypt, God's people had been looking in many directions to get their daily needs met. They looked down at crops growing from the land. They looked out at the available livestock for meat. And they looked to their Egyptian slave masters in order to be told when they could eat and how much they could eat. It seems like the Israelites were conditioned to look everywhere for their provision — everywhere except up.

Looking down and around was the opposite of looking up to God. It was the opposite of trusting God to be their provider.

A NOTE FROM JOEL

The Egyptians had the Israelites working to construct all kinds of buildings, like temples and palaces. In order to keep watch over them, the Egyptian taskmasters stood on platforms and looked down on the Israelites as they worked. Platforms are always so deceptive because they make us feel bigger, better and more powerful than we actually are. Just think about our day and age with the platforms of social media. With every like, comment and share on Instagram it can feel like our platform is being built brick by brick (or like by like!). This is an important reminder for us not to look down at what we create but rather look up at what God provides

So, when God delivered Israel from Egypt and into the wilderness, those provisions and slave masters weren't there anymore. The Israelites were no longer slaves. They were technically free. But as long as their routines were chained to old habits, old thinking and old activities, they wouldn't ever experience real freedom.

And God was brilliant in working on the heart and mindset change they needed by using their most basic, daily need — food. He took them out to the desert, where they would not be able to look down at the land or out to the herds or over to their slave masters to get their needs met.

They would have to look up.

Lysa here. My morning prayer each day includes a portion where I acknowledge my need to look to and look for God every day. "God, show me someone to forgive, someone to bless, and help me actively look all around me for Your goodness and faithfulness." In other words, I know God is my provider. But I want to attribute to God the provision I experience each day so that I acknowledge His presence and activity in my daily life. Walking daily with God helps me to more quickly remember that God will be my provider in the bigger things. And even more importantly, it helps me trust Him to provide when the really hard times come as well.

01 | How can you start practicing looking up to God more often for your daily provision?

02 Read Exodus 16:4. What does God say?

Israel's food would come from Him and Him alone. He would rain down just enough bread each day to sustain them. They would have to develop a new daily habit, new thinking and new activities in order to get their food. They were no longer slaves to a master in Egypt. They would have to learn to look to God for everything in the wilderness.

But real transformation won't occur with just an external relocation. It requires a complete internal renovation. And isn't it interesting that God says He will use their basic need of food, and His unique way of providing it, to test and see if His people will follow His instructions? Like we said earlier, it can make us feel vulnerable to feel the emptiness of an unmet need.

03 Read Exodus 16:31. What type of bread God was going to provide for His people?

The story of this bread from heaven, or manna, in Exodus was a gift. In fact, it was a gracious gift because it came in an unexpected way. Can you imagine seeing bread fall from heaven?! Also, manna was an opportunity. Every time the Israelites went out in the morning to gather the bread that fell from heaven, they were given an opportunity to look up to God and acknowledge Him as their provider. Doing this daily was crucial so the Israelites could develop new patterns of trusting God in both their thinking and their actions.

In Exodus 16:4, we are reminded that the One in heaven who provides rain, which is essential for life to be sustained long term, is also the One who sends bread, which sustains life daily! The manna coming from heaven was the fulfillment of God's promise to the Israelites. His presence and provision in their daily moments of need was also intended to train them to expect God to intervene and act in the same way with their future needs. (Exodus 16:1-8)

After 40 years of being in the desert and eating the manna from heaven that the Lord provided, the Israelites had a pretty good understanding of how the process worked. Six days of the week, the Lord would provide manna. However, there would be no bread on the seventh day, for it was the Sabbath. Instead, the Israelites were to collect a double portion on the sixth day so they would have enough for two days. They were not to try to stockpile the manna. It was given to them daily so they would remember to trust in God alone to provide for them.

Then we get to Exodus 16:32: *"Moses said, 'This is what the LORD has commanded: "Take an omer of manna and keep it for generations to come, so they can see the bread I gave you to eat in the wilderness when I brought you out of Egypt"'"* (NIV).

For years the Israelites were not allowed to keep any extra manna, but now they were commanded to keep an omer: the exact amount that was used for one day's provision. We see something so sincere from God's heart in this request. He wanted His people to have something to remind them that He alone would always be their Provider.

Visual reminders are good for all of us. These reminders help us when we forget about all of the ways God has been faithful to provide for us over the years.

The manna in the Old Testament was intended to stir anticipation for a manna that would be eternal in nature. In other words, the manna of the Old Testament was an intentional symbol for intermediate provision until the Manna from heaven came to bring true and eternal satisfaction. This is in fact the best kind of provision we could ask for: the Bread of Life. Jesus Himself.

In John 6:31-35, Jesus declares Himself as the Bread of Life. He makes a direct connection to Moses and the story of the manna in the wilderness. The Jews hearing Jesus, who were steeped in the story of the Old Testament, must have known this story well. Manna was the literal bread that saved their ancestors from impending death. Just as the ancient Israelites were taught to live a 24-hour cycle of reliance on Yahweh to provide the bread from heaven, Jesus reminds us there is something even better we can rely on 24 hours a day ... Himself.

Jesus said it best:

"'For the bread of God is he who comes down from heaven and gives life to the world.' They said to him, 'Sir, give us this bread always.' Jesus said to them, 'I am the bread of life; whoever comes to me shall not hunger, and whoever believes in me shall never thirst.'" (John 6:33-35)

Here are some final takeaways about Jesus as the Bread of Life and our Ultimate Provider:

• **Trusting in Jesus as the Bread of Life grows our dependence on Him for the *daily bread* we ask for.**

When Jesus taught us to pray in Matthew 6, He said, *"Give us this day our daily bread ..."* (v. 11). The Greek word for "daily" (ἐπιούσιον) can be best understood in this context as referring to the present but also the days to come.[50] So when we read Jesus' request for daily bread in the Lord's Prayer, we are invited to pray in hopeful anticipation for the future (the heavenly banquet) but also pray to be sustained by God's perfect provision in the present (manna).

When we remember Jesus is the Bread of Life as we pray for daily bread, we grow in dependence and trust in Him when life feels confusing. And when what we see in front of us isn't what we thought it would look like — even when we don't agree that this is good — we don't have to understand God to trust Him.

- **Knowing Jesus as the Bread of Life creates an even deeper moment of meaning for us when we break bread during Communion.**

In Luke 22:14-20 Jesus is reclining at a table and tells His disciples to remember, whenever they break bread in Communion, that the bread is a symbol of His body. Jesus connects and completes the image of manna as provision for the people of God in the wilderness, as His own body would be broken as a type of provision for all of humanity, for all those who repent of their sin and turn to Him. The people in the wilderness would wake up hungry and looking for bread the next day, but the person who remembers the body of Jesus, broken for them, will be reminded of the fullness of sacrifice, and as Jesus said, they will hunger and thirst no longer. (John 6:35)

- **Remembering Jesus as the Bread of Life can comfort us in our own experiences of lack and longing.**

God showed His faithfulness by sending bread from heaven. The people lived out their faithfulness and dependence on God by walking out every day and gathering the bread. They had a part to play. Sometimes I think we can easily neglect that relationships require responses from both parties. God always acts, responds and reacts. The question is never about the faithfulness and action of God. It is and always has been about our willingness to respond and react to the goodness that God extends to us. Friends, the greatest goodness that God sent us, the most fulfilling provision we could ever experience, is Jesus. But where did Jesus come from? Heaven.

As we've studied parts of the Old Testament, we have seen so many glimpses of Jesus. At times we may have felt that these glimpses have been limited. Typically, when this happens it is because our vision is blurred by factors such as trauma, relationship complications, betrayal, abandonment, financial hardships, fear, anxiety about world events, and our own skepticism. But God is building something we cannot even begin to fathom, much less see. We don't serve a "do nothing" God. God is always doing something.

Now, His provision may not be as obvious as we want it to be. Or it may not come to us looking exactly like we expected. The Israelites certainly didn't expect bread to look like little sweet potato flakes falling from heaven (manna). And the timing of His provision may seem slow. We may see it in due time or maybe not until eternity. During the 40 years the Israelites were in the desert, they didn't get the big, bountiful meals they wanted. That didn't come until they finally crossed over into the promised land. But God's provision was all around them each morning when the manna fell from heaven. The same is true for us. Jesus is all around us, providing for us on a daily basis. We can trust with certainty that whatever He gives us today truly is His good and perfect provision for right now. And whether that provision is what we want right now or it's a part of a much bigger plan for our eventual good, it's still good.

God is providing. Jesus is <u>FAITHFULLY</u> with us in *all* of our needs.
We are cared for. That has been the *pattern* of <u>DIVINE PROVISION</u>
since the <u>BEGINNING</u> of time. And we can take comfort in the
fact that this will *never change.*

PROVISION REVEALED IN WATER FROM A ROCK AND A ROD

To close out this week's study on provisions, we're going to look into the life of Moses. Although we've talked about Moses in a broader sense, we're going to hone in on some crucial moments in his life that will help us see the provision of God in anticipation and awareness for when we see Jesus. The picture we will see in the Old Testament story is supposed to be a picture that is almost out of focus. But the picture becomes clearer when seen through the lens of Jesus. In this way we find the presence of Jesus in the Old Testament more clearly.

As we begin today, think about the word *need*. When we hear that word, just like we talked about yesterday with people's hunger, there is an urgency and an angst. Today, we are going to look at the crucial need every human has for water.

People often feel the most vulnerable in the area of their greatest need.

Perhaps the deepest vulnerability comes with unmet, daily physical needs like hunger and thirst. For example, one of our most vital daily needs is water. We can't last more than a few days without it. For the Israelites in the wilderness, when water seemed out of reach, they surely felt deprived and desperate.

It's clear from Scripture that the place we feel the most vulnerable … the place of our greatest need … is right where God will meet us. Our desperation creates an opportunity for a divine appointment where God can reveal Himself to us and provide for our needs.

01 In what area of your life are you feeling vulnerable right now because of something you need? Is it hard for you to be honest with God about what you need?

Let's look at two examples of God providing water for the people of Israel. The first is found in Exodus 17.

Read Exodus 17:1-4.

By this point in their exodus journey, the Israelites had only been traveling for a few weeks in the desert wilderness. Up to this point, they'd seen God provide for their basic needs on countless occasions, even in the most desperate situations. Yet they turned from trusting in God to tormenting Moses with their quarrelsome and ungrateful words and behavior.

With that in mind, pay attention to the details of God's words as He responds, beginning in Exodus 17:5:

"And the LORD said to Moses, 'Pass on before the people, taking with you some of the elders of Israel, and take in your hand the staff with which you struck the Nile, and go. Behold, I will stand before you there on the rock at Horeb, and you shall strike the rock, and water shall come out of it, and the people will drink.' And Moses did so, in the sight of the elders of Israel. And he called the name of the place Massah and Meribah, because of the quarreling of the people of Israel, and because they tested the LORD by saying, 'Is the LORD among us or not?'" (Exodus 17:5-7)

— A NOTE FROM JOEL

The literal translation of "Massah" is "testing," and "Meribah" means "quarreling."

Let's go to a previous time when the Lord instructed Moses to use his staff. Interestingly, when the children of Israel were still being held captive in Egypt, God specifically tells Moses to use a "staff" (or rod) to strike the Nile and turn it into blood. This was the first of the 10 plagues God used to make Pharaoh aware of God's superior power. Let's look back at Exodus 7:20.

Moses and Aaron obeyed God, and the Nile did indeed turn to blood. As we compare the stories in Exodus 7:20 and Exodus 17:5-7, we find an important connection with these two situations through the staff Moses used.

As the Israelites demanded water in Exodus 17, God reminded both Moses and the people that the very staff that struck the Nile and turned it to blood, causing immense death, would now be used by God to provide water and sustain life. Moses was then told to strike the rock that would provide water for the people.

God's faithfulness in providing for His people's thirst held great potential for deeper trust between them. But the people of God started wavering when God didn't immediately show them an obvious water supply. They suddenly wanted to go back to Egypt where the water supply was easier to get, and they started reframing the brutality of their past slavery as safe and secure. (Exodus 16:3)

— A NOTE FROM JOEL

The Nile River was the source of life for the Egyptians and a key location of stability and provision for the Ancient Near Eastern world. The Nile also had a long history with the Israelites. The Nile was the place where the male children of Israel were killed by Pharaoh. (Exodus 1:22) The Nile was also the place where Moses was rescued as a baby. (Exodus 2:1-10) The Nile was the place of both life and death.

Even though God took the people out of Egypt, the process of getting Egypt out of the people was going to require more than just a physical relocation. They were physically free. But they were not mentally free. Their constant doubt, lack of trust, and confusion about timing, looking back as if Egypt wasn't as bad as it really was, created further chaos for them in everything, including their relationship with God.

Now let's look at a second example of God providing water for His people, found in Numbers 20.

Read Numbers 20:1-5.

"And the people of Israel, the whole congregation, came into the wilderness of Zin in the first month, and the people stayed in Kadesh. And Miriam died there and was buried there. Now there was no water for the congregation. And they assembled themselves together against Moses and against Aaron. And the people quarreled with Moses and said, 'Would that we had perished when our brothers perished before the LORD! Why have you brought the assembly of the LORD into this wilderness, that we should die here, both we and our cattle? And why have you made us come up out of Egypt to bring us to this evil place? It is no place for grain or figs or vines or pomegranates, and there is no water to drink.'"

Sound familiar? But notice God's instruction to Moses here in these passages was different than the first time God told Moses to get water from the rock back in Exodus.

02 | Read Numbers 20:6-9. What are God's directions to Moses?

03 | Now read Numbers 20:10-13. What did Moses do instead?

There are so many possibilities of why Moses struck the rock instead of speaking to it. Previously, in Exodus 17, God had instructed Moses to strike the rock. But in this moment, God instructed Moses to speak to the rock. Moses' act of disobedience actually places him in the same state of rebellion as the quarrelsome Israelites. There is something important for us to notice here. God wants us to follow His day-by-day direction rather than slipping into a pattern of just using past instructions from Him. God knows what we need today and wants us to be in relationship with Him so He can lead us in what's best for each situation we face. Just because He spoke and directed us in one way in the past, this does not mean He will always do that same thing in the future. God leads; we follow. That's the pattern we should commit to.

The rod and the rock were both present in these stories (Exodus 17 and Numbers 20). The rod would strike the rock, and water would flow from the rock. In other words, provision for the people would come through an act of aggression. However, the same object that is the victim of the aggression (the rock) is the source of the provision.

The Apostle Paul's words bring fulfillment to the image of the rock and the rod in a profound way in 1 Corinthians 10:1-4. Paul reflects on the story of the Israelites in the wilderness, identifying the rock of Exodus 17 and Numbers 20 as *Christ Himself.*

This is a mind-blowing connection that again helps us notice that the picture of the rock and the rod in these Old Testament stories was always intended to help us see a glimpse of Jesus.

In Matthew 27:29-30, Jesus is struck (becoming a victim of aggression) as He is led away to be crucified. Jesus would be hung on the cross so that ultimately, through the pouring out of His very own blood, He would both physically and spiritually save all who place their trust in Him. Paul is teaching us how to read and understand the story of Jesus in the New Testament through the lens and narrative of the Old Testament.

But seeing Jesus inside these stories doesn't just end there. In John 7:37-52, we find Jesus not providing a physical source for water but declaring that He **Himself** is bringing the Living Water of God. He was declaring, just like He has over and over again through the revelations and connections we've studied together, that all of the Old Testament scriptures point to *Him*.

We all have a physical thirst. Our thirst is an indication that our body needs water. But Jesus is speaking to an even deeper thirst we all have: the thirst in our soul that nothing else can ever satisfy. And the way we access satisfaction or even relief from this spiritual thirst is not by working harder to get to God ... No, instead, Living Water came to us. And the only thing He requires from us is that we recognize our deep need for Him and, in response, turn to Him.

04 | Think about the spiritual thirst we just talked about. What do you find your soul really thirsting for? What do you so desperately desire? Write out a prayer inviting Jesus into this need.

The stories of the Old Testament, especially these two stories that deal with rocks and a rod, don't just reveal Jesus to us; they also remind us of God's faithfulness with our own deep longings and needs.

In the wilderness, God provided water for the Israelites. And even better, God provided, through Jesus, Living Water for anyone who would come and confess their thirst and need for eternal satisfaction. Even when we have unmet and unfulfilled longings, He has forever made a way. And while we're in the wilderness of living with all the imperfections and devastations of a world full of sin, we will never go thirsty when we trust in Jesus. We all long for the perfection of heaven to invade earth, but while we wait, let's keep turning to Jesus, our only connection to perfection and satisfaction here in this world. The Living Water available to us today is yet an appetizer of what is to come.

As we conclude this week, let's meditate on these thoughts as we read Revelation 21:1-7 and pray together: *Father God, thank You so much for sending Your Son, Jesus, as the ultimate Prophet, Priest, King, Bread of Life and Living Water. Seeing Him so active and evident in Scripture brings me such comfort in places of my heart that feel empty today. Thank You for listening to my prayers for all the things I desire, need, want and ask for. I pray, in the meantime, You sustain my faith by reminding me of Your past faithfulness to always keep Your promises. Thank You for the perfect provision of Jesus that paved the way for a relationship with You. In Jesus' Name, Amen.*

WEEK *five*

THROUGH PROTECTIONS

INTRODUCTION TO PROTECTIONS

Lysa here. Since we're all friends now by Week 5 of the study, I just need to give you a little peek inside my brain. I'm a happy and positive person mostly. But when I get afraid, I can think of worst-case scenarios quicker than just about anyone I know. It's not that I get doomsday-ish. I just want to brace myself for all possible outcomes of a situation. Now, granted, in some cases being aware of possible dangers can help me take appropriate extra precautions. But letting my fears go unchecked can make me feel like I'm in a constant state of threat and emergency.

As I've watched this play out in my life, here's what I've learned: Collecting worst-case scenarios doesn't protect me. It only projects the possible pain of tomorrow into today and feeds more fear. And really, what it reveals to me is this: I have trouble trusting God as my ultimate protector.

If you struggle with this too, I think you're going to find these next few days very helpful. Interestingly enough, using various images throughout the Old Testament, God is referred to as a protector. We see Him referred to as a fortress, (Psalm 18:2) shield, (2 Samuel 22:31) hiding place, (Psalm 32:7) refuge, (Psalm 91:2) shelter (Isaiah 25:4) and stronghold. (Nahum 1:7) These visual images are based on real places in Old Testament times that offered safe harbor in the midst of danger. A place to run when chaos threatened. They were also symbols of promised protection when things were peaceful. If there was ever any doubt about safety and security, these symbols and images served as a source of reassurance and were places of security and peace, to rest and recover.

The people of Israel needed physical places like these as protection from enemies, which is why so many cities had walls. Though we don't have walled cities with high towers for protection, we have symbols of protection all around us today. Some houses have fences. Even walking through security at the airport reminds us that safety is a precaution and a priority. However, these security measures can only protect us to a certain extent. Ultimately, we need a God who offers His protection.

Thankfully our Divine Warrior is still fighting on our behalf. He hasn't abandoned His role as our protector. But His protection doesn't always look the same today as it did for the Israelites.

Sometimes we experience hardship and harm as a result of sin, both ours and others', and in these moments we may wonder where God's protection is. We may look back at our lives and declare that God surely abandoned us in a time of greatest need. And if that's you, please know I get it. I sometimes have those same feelings as well.

Trying to understand and trust God as our protector, in the midst of a very fallen world, can be confusing and scary. In fact, it's one of the greatest areas of spiritual wrestling we will ever do. Even "giants" of our faith struggled with this paradox.

— A NOTE FROM JOEL

The psalms are filled with David's heartfelt cries of abandonment and fears around being so vulnerable to his enemies. In Psalm 13:1, David cries out, *"How long, O LORD? Will you forget me forever? How long will you hide your face from me?"*

The north African church father Augustine wrote one of his most influential works, *City of God*, as he wrestled with these very realities.

But as we will see this week, God's protection comes in many forms — it's not always a physical removal of threat or a relief of emotional pain. Sometimes His protection is spiritual. Spiritual protection is what God is doing in the spiritual realm that we don't see. With everything we go through, there is what we see right in front of us. But at the same time, there is a battle in the spiritual realm. Remember Ephesians 6:12: *"For our struggle is not against flesh and blood, but against the rulers, against the authorities, against the powers of this dark world and against the spiritual forces of evil in the heavenly realms"* (NIV).

Throughout so many stories we've studied together, we've seen evidence eventually confirm that God was working things out in unseen ways. What first appeared to be God not rescuing someone in the short-run wound up ending differently. God was working behind the scenes for their protection in the long-run. God is never a do-nothing God. And the greatest assurance of that spiritual protection is found in Jesus Himself, who can see what is happening in both the physical and the spiritual realms at the same time and who is leading us, guiding us and standing with us through it all.

Joel here. So, no matter what's scaring us today, we can be confident God's protection for humanity is always secure in the spiritual protection we have in Jesus Himself. I also think it's important here to pause and acknowledge how hard this is. We may wonder how the "spiritual protection" of Jesus makes any difference in our present, right-now life. Sometimes the answer we want isn't necessarily the answer we get in the Bible. This may frustrate us; it definitely frustrates me. But I also don't want to miss that this aspect of the Bible is also what makes the Scriptures reliable. The Bible doesn't tell us what we want to hear but what we need to receive.

It's true — sometimes we don't get the physical protection we desire. It's also true that the sun shines on the sinner and the saint alike. Rain falls on both the just and unjust. (Matthew 5:45) Bad things sadly do happen to good people. Evil people do at times prosper. It's also important to remember the reality that our earthly experiences are but a moment in the context of eternity. The hope of Christ is the new heavens AND new earth. It's a future where heaven and earth meet, and all things return to that edenic vision of Genesis 1. The spiritual protection we receive from Jesus is an assurance that we will also experience a future full of physical and spiritual protection in the Kingdom of God. In other words, the comfort we receive today comes from the assurance of a future where things will change because Jesus is trustworthy.

This spiritual protection is unshakable. When we turn to God, we can count on Him to draw us near, to heal our wounds and strengthen our hearts. God will use even the darkest situations as a catalyst to show His strength as our eternal protector.

And then, when God does provide for our physical and emotional needs, we can delight in those moments. But when we don't tangibly experience God's physical or emotional protection, we can always be assured of His spiritual protection that Christ secured for us on the cross.

This week, we'll take a look at God's actions throughout Scripture that show His caring nature and how He steps in to protect His people. Then, as we study God's protection throughout the Old Testament, we'll start to see each of these moments in Scripture as a step towards the ultimate protection we have in Christ Jesus.

It's fascinating to learn that some people in the Old Testament serve as shadows and types of the greater Protector to come: Jesus. These people were hand-picked by God, which was demonstrated in unusual, unexplainable, unlikely and unique ways but always ended in unchanging protection for the Israelites.

If you are a highlighting kind of person, mark these five words: unusual, unexplainable, unlikely, unique and unchanging. Those words will be important in the new perspectives we will gain this week around God's protection and how we can more clearly see Jesus in the midst of it all.

First, we will take another look at Joseph, examining some different facets of his story than we did in Week 3. Though Joseph had been savagely abandoned by his brothers, God used all Joseph learned in his years of suffering to give him the wisdom and discernment he would eventually need to help save the lives of God's people and the entire nation of Egypt as well. Joseph's pain was not pointless, but it was an unusual way God demonstrated His protection for Joseph and all His people. If we can keep this in mind today, we can remember that, though we will experience suffering here in this world, it will not be for nothing. God uses what we go through to draw our hearts to Jesus, who also suffered here on earth and became the ultimate protector and savior of our souls. And God often uses us to help ease the suffering of others when we share the hope we have found in Jesus and what we've learned through our hardships.

Second, God also sometimes intervenes immediately to supernaturally protect His people. We see this when He protected Moses and the Israelites from total devastation at the Red Sea, when Pharaoh and the Egyptians were chasing them. The Red Sea parted for the Israelites but then closed over and drowned their enemies, the Egyptians. Let's be honest — this is totally unexplainable and so incredibly supernatural that we are still talking about this event in history today.

The memory of Yahweh's protection at the Red Sea was meant to be embedded into the hearts and minds of the Israelites back then and even us today! The events at the Red Sea provided the Israelites (and us) a perspective shift. The very thing that could bring total defeat and disaster (the sea) ended up being used by God to provide protection. This should help us with some perspective shifts in our own lives. We are to remember that, while a great deliverance took place when God parted the waters, a greater deliverance and protection was and still is to come through Jesus.

In the Old Testament we also find that God sometimes uses unlikely ways to protect us, such as Jonah being swallowed by a large fish and rescuing the Ninevites, who were enemies of God. Situations like this remind us that sometimes God's protection won't be seen as protection in the short-term so we must look for it long-term.

In addition, Scripture reveals God has a very special and specific care for the poor and powerless. As God establishes His Kingdom on earth, we see His intentional protection of the orphan, widow and those on the margins of society. In fact, in passages like Micah 6:8, the people of God are called upon to be agents of protection to the powerless. Failure to do so was, and is, a grave sin.

This week as we study, we will find that God works in unusual, unexplainable, unlikely, unique and unchanging ways to protect those He loves. Who does God love? The people He created in His likeness and image ... including you and me. Each day we will gain greater revelations of God's goodness through His protection and find that Jesus was at the center of each of these moments, in either visible or hidden ways. Regardless, He was there. And if He was there in those moments, we can be assured that Jesus is with us in the moments when we need His protection.

DAY TWENTY-ONE

THE UNUSUAL PROTECTION OF JOSEPH

Lysa here. I like God's protection to be completely obvious and immediate. And I believe this can cause me to miss seeing His protection and wrongly think He's not there for me. That's why looking at the story of Joseph again is very helpful.

We've already looked at the big picture of Joseph's life and some of the pretty extreme betrayals, heartbreaks and traumas he went through. But today, I want to take a more focused look at the shift he made from being wounded to protecting the very family members who harmed him the most.

This is another example of how the story of Joseph creates a connection to Jesus. Jesus also experienced relational wounding, abandonment, betrayal and rejection by the very ones He eventually saved. The people projected their own issues onto the very One who would eventually protect them in life-saving ways.

I don't want us to miss the fact that Joseph is a person, not just a character in a story. Some of the very same reactions we have to our pain must have been there for Joseph as well. The fear, anxiety, uncertainties, weeping, worrying about all the worst-case scenarios and trying to stay hopeful when every circumstance around him just seemed to point to hopelessness. If I let my mind sit in some of the details of Joseph's devastations, I can relate to him so very much even though our stories are unfolding thousands of years apart.

I imagine he woke up in the middle of the night feeling panicked sometimes.

I imagine he felt incredibly isolated and alone in his pain.

I imagine he questioned why God wasn't intervening by preventing some of the horrors he faced.

I imagine he worried that God had forgotten or abandoned him.

I imagine he wondered if anyone would ever rise up to defend, help and protect him.

I imagine he doubted that any of this could ever really be used for good.

Yes, I really can relate to Joseph so much. But what I'm especially curious about is how he shifted his perspective from being consumed with the unfairness of it all to trusting God with the unfolding of it all.

First, let's look at a place in Scripture where Joseph speaks about the unfairness and angst of what's happened to him while still in prison. Read Genesis 40:15.

01 | How do you relate to this statement from Joseph?

Next read Genesis 41:1 and then verses 39-40. This happens two years after Joseph spoke the statement about not deserving to be in this prison. Two long years where I'm sure Joseph once again felt abandoned and so incredibly hopeless. And then, in a moment, everything turns around: *"... Pharaoh sent for Joseph, and he was quickly brought from the dungeon"* (Genesis 41:14a, NIV). In this crucial conversation Joseph has with Pharaoh, something incredible happens.

When Pharaoh asks Joseph if he can interpret his dream, Joseph says no. I find this astounding because this was his big moment to shine in front of the very one who had the power to change everything about Joseph's dire situation! Instead Joseph puts his faith in God on display: *"'I cannot do it,' Joseph replied to Pharaoh, 'but God will give Pharaoh the answer he desires'"* (Genesis 41:16, NIV). After interpreting Pharaoh's dreams, Joseph impresses him so much with his wisdom and discernment that Joseph is promoted to become the second-most-powerful man in Egypt.

When it may have seemed like, for years, God wasn't there for him, as Joseph's story unfolds, we can see something different. God had absolutely been working through the hardships of Joseph to develop in him everything he would need to step into a calling that would save many lives. Joseph gained wisdom and discernment greater than any Pharaoh had seen in anyone else.

02 | As you think about some of your hardships right now, what good qualities might God be developing in you through what you are facing?

God wasn't just developing Joseph's character. He would use what Joseph went through to be an eventual massive protection for the people of Egypt and the Israelites as well.

03 | How does Joseph's story help you see the possibility for a perspective shift in God's protection? How could some part of what you're walking through be part of an unlikely protection from God?

Now, read Genesis 45:1-8. This is the moment when Joseph no longer hides his identity from his brothers. Pay close attention to the perspective shift Joseph reveals in verses 5 and 8. Not only is he starting to see his experience as God's unlikely way of protecting him, but he's also seeing some greater purpose as well.

04 | What was the greater purpose of Joseph's pain? How does this encourage you to also look for some purpose in your pain?

The story of Joseph is used to teach us so much about God's character and faithfulness. God's protection really does sometimes come in unlikely ways that we might misunderstand. Instead of being tempted to wrongly think God is being cruel or uncaring, maybe we can believe He's developing our character to prepare us for a much bigger protection than we can fathom.

Lysa here. A verse I love to speak over many situations I've been facing lately is Genesis 50:20, where Joseph speaks these words to his brothers: *"As for you, you meant evil against me, but God meant it for good, to bring it about that many people should be kept alive, as they are today."*

Now, before we throw a celebration of all the good we can learn from Joseph, I think it's valuable to also learn from some not-so-good choices he made. This lesson is a warning to us all.

While Joseph demonstrated great faith in God, after he was delivered from prison and put in a place of authority, some of his past weaknesses crept back up. It is totally possible to have great faith *in God* and yet still struggle with being fully submitted *to God*. Some of those same tendencies to be prideful and self-serving, which Joseph demonstrated at 17 years old (see Genesis 37:1-11), resurfaced. But this time, instead of just fueling the jealousy of his brothers by bragging about his dreams, he used his position of power in harsh ways. Instead of caring for both his people and the people of Egypt with equal measures of compassion, he was sometimes cruel and harsh with the Egyptians.

It wasn't that Joseph was blatantly sinning, but he acted in ways that weren't in line with the compassion he should have extended toward others. All the people in Egypt were suffering from the same severe conditions. Joseph personally knew extreme suffering since he'd gone through very traumatizing situations in his past. But when entrusted with a position of power to help demonstrate compassion to all, he sometimes showed favoritism to the Israelites and was unfairly harsh with the Egyptians.

Let's pick back up with his story in Genesis 46, where we see an example of this cruelty with the Egyptians. Take a close look at Genesis 46:31-34. Keep in mind this is later in Joseph's story when he's finally reunited with his father, Jacob, who thought Joseph had died years before.

05 | What is Joseph's plan to protect his family while they live in Egypt?

At this point in Joseph's story, he is governing Egypt with full authority, (Genesis 41:40) and his father, his brothers and their families have finally arrived from the land of Canaan as honored guests.

Initially, it looks like Joseph is simply being strategic and giving his brothers the best advice in order to ensure that they are taken care of in Egypt (protection). But as we will see, there seems to be another motive, which will have grave consequences for future generations of Israelites. However, the immediate consequences for Joseph's brothers and their family turn out great.

Read Genesis 47:1-6.

Joseph sets up his brothers and his people in the best land (Goshen), where they care for their own livestock as well as all the livestock that belong to Pharaoh. Joseph shows care, compassion and kindness and works to ensure that his family is protected and their needs are met.

During this time, the Israelites prosper and God fulfills the promise He made to Jacob: *"And God spoke to Israel in visions of the night and said, 'Jacob, Jacob.' And he said, 'Here I am.' Then he said, 'I am God, the God of your father. Do not be afraid to go down to Egypt, for there I will make you into a great nation. I myself will go down with you to Egypt, and I will also bring you up again, and Joseph's hand shall close your eyes'"* (Genesis 46:2-4).

Everything is going as planned. Joseph is thriving and God's people are thriving. Joseph has every reason to be generous with the nation that has enabled all this thriving. We would expect, maybe even hope, that Joseph would show the Egyptians the same empathy, love and compassion he shows to the Israelites. But Joseph's treatment of the Egyptians in the midst of a famine shows us a different side of Joseph.

06 | Read Genesis 47:13-20. Summarize what Joseph chooses to do. What might his motivations have been?

Notice how Joseph deals with the Egyptians. He takes their money in exchange for food. When they have no more money, he asks for their livestock in exchange for food. Now, who takes care of the livestock? Oh yeah, Joseph's family! At this point we would expect Joseph to show compassion and extend generosity, giving the Egyptians what they need. After all, that's what God intended to take place through Pharaoh's dreams and Joseph's interpretation of the dreams. (Genesis 41) But Joseph goes on to take Egyptian people's land and enslaves many of the Egyptians themselves in exchange for food. (Genesis 47:19-21)

07 | Have you ever been blessed by God's protection and provision and had an opportunity to do good for someone else, without conditions ... but didn't? What were the consequences of that choice?

It's true Joseph did provide for the Egyptians by having food available for purchase, and he did an excellent job in administration. However, when it came to protecting and caring for the people, Joseph strategically orchestrated the situation to put the Israelites in a better position.

08 | What do you see in Joseph's character that would lead him to prioritize the Israelites at the expense of the Egyptians?

It's no wonder Genesis 47:27 tells us that Israel settled in Egypt and was fruitful and multiplied greatly. But it's also no longer as surprising that there came a time years later when the Egyptians turned against the Israelites and made them slaves. When many years had passed and a pharaoh came into power who did not know Joseph, the pharaoh grew fearful of the Israelites and their great numbers. The result? He enslaved the entire nation of Israel and treated them in harsh and cruel ways. We can't help but wonder if maybe a significant weakness in Joseph's actions fed some bitterness in the Egyptians that eventually hurt Joseph's descendants in huge ways.

Now, here's where we can see Jesus, the greater Joseph, offer protection to all people who turn to Him without carrying any bias or prejudice or personal agenda. This is where we can learn from the example of Jesus, who gives us a better way.

Let's look at Hebrews 5:2 and verses 7-9. The author of Hebrews tells us that Jesus in His humanity learned obedience through His suffering. Never forget, like we already said in Week 4, while Jesus was sinless, He knew well the pain of being sinned against. Ultimately, as these verses point out, the weakness, suffering and obedience of Jesus leads Him to deal gently with us. The Greek word for "learned" (ἔμαθεν) in Hebrews 5:8 suggests a process.[51] I think this is so comforting for us to pause and consider. Jesus didn't simply arrive without enduring affliction. He willingly submitted Himself to the process that would lead to suffering. But the suffering and weakness of Jesus resulted in a deep awareness and empathy for the hardship of those around Him. Joseph falls short in his kindness and compassion, but Jesus models it with perfection. The gentleness and kindness of Jesus can be seen because Jesus extends salvation to all people who obey Him.

This is another area where Jesus is the greater Joseph. Jesus lived a life of perfection and endured pain and suffering not for just one people group or ethnicity but for all people groups and ethnicities. Jesus' death, burial, resurrection and ascension is an act of redemptive reversal. Unlike Joseph, who enslaved those who were not his own, Jesus redeems, restores and reclaims all people who turn from their sin and turn towards Him as the Messiah.

This is exactly what Paul says in Galatians 4:3-7: *"In the same way we also, when we were children, were enslaved to the elementary principles of the world. But when the fullness of time had come, God sent forth his Son, born of woman, born under the law, to redeem those who were under the law, so that we might receive adoption as sons. And because you are sons, God has sent the Spirit of his Son into our hearts, crying, 'Abba! Father!' So you are no longer a slave, but a son, and if a son, then an heir through God."*

09 | Has Jesus ever redeemed/restored/released you from any form of "captivity"? Things that hold us captive can be thought processes, fears, addictions, etc. How have you experienced God's protection in this way?

Joseph looked out for his own family, but Jesus made a way for all to be invited and included into the family of God. Not only have we been set free from the bondage of sin, but we were also granted the status of sons of God. Jesus does for you and I what Joseph could never do. Jesus elevates us as royal children of the King of heaven and earth. The great promise of this adoption by God, as Paul says in these verses, is that the Spirit of Jesus was sent to us as a sign and symbol of our future inheritance.

DAY TWENTY-TWO

THE UNEXPLAINABLE PROTECTION IN THE RED SEA

Trust is delicate. It's hard to earn and easy to lose. Trusting someone else takes time. Especially when it comes to our own protection. We were designed with a high level of awareness around our need for self-protection, and at the slightest threat, we fight, fly or freeze.

If someone breaks our trust, we naturally get guarded. If someone breaks our trust over and over, we may need to avoid them or end the relationship altogether.

Lysa here. I've said it before and I'll say it again: Trust is the oxygen of human relationships. Without it, relationships die. But with trust, our relationships can flourish. When someone proves they are trustworthy, our confidence in them grows and we feel safe enough to let our guard down. Why? Because when there is a consistent pattern of faithfulness demonstrated in the past, we can feel safe trusting someone with whatever we are facing today.

I believe this is the kind of trust Moses had developed with God. He could trace God's past faithful protection over and over. Moses had seen God help him do what he thought would be completely impossible: leading the Israelites out of captivity in Egypt. Just when there seemed to be no way Pharaoh would ever heed Moses' demand to let the people go, God demonstrated His *unexplainable* protection by using His power over nature to get Pharaoh's attention. God unleashed 10 plagues over Egypt, which eventually convinced Pharaoh to let the Israelites go.

Then God demonstrated His unexplainable protection again when He led the people in a less direct path to the promised land: *"But God led the people around by the way of the wilderness toward the Red Sea"* (Exodus 13:18a).

Exodus 14:4 reveals God's plan to yet again show His people His ability to protect them: *"'And I will harden Pharaoh's heart, and he will pursue them, and I will get glory over Pharaoh and all his host, and the Egyptians shall know that I am the Lord.' And they did so."*

Just as God planned, with the Egyptians marching after them, the Israelites found themselves facing an angry sea in front of them and an angry enemy behind them. The only way for them to be saved would be for God to do something that could never have even been dreamed up with the human mind ... Again it was God's *unexplainable* protection.

Let's pause the story there and take a look at the wording the writer of Exodus used for the body of water in front of God's people. In the original Hebrew, the "Red Sea" is actually the "Sea of Reeds." In fact, the Hebrew word *(sûp⁻)* in Exodus 13:18, which is translated as "red" in most English translations of the Bible, is literally "reed" and is the same word used in Exodus 2:3 and Exodus 2:5.

Read Exodus 2:3-5.

This section of Scripture recounts the story of Moses in a basket in the Nile River (the same river where Pharaoh ordered the murder of Jewish male children, referenced in Exodus 1:22) and explains the importance of the reeds. In an unexplainable turn of events, it is in this blood-stained river that God protects Moses and catches him up in reeds to be found by Pharaoh's daughter. Here's where we start to see the connection between "reeds" and "red."

Let's go back to the question of why our English translations say "Red Sea." Well, some may say the very first commentary of the Old Testament is the "Septuagint," or the Greek translation of the Hebrew Old Testament. In the Septuagint, the translators made a conscious decision to translate the Hebrew "reed" into the Greek word ἐρυθρὰν, which translates as "red."

— A NOTE FROM JOEL

Here's a quick definition for "commentary": a resource that provides an explanation or a unique perspective on the Bible.

In order to understand this decision, let's take a look at the rest of the story.

Read Exodus 14:10-12.

01 | What does the people's response to Moses show about their mental and emotional state?

Notice a common thread in the reaction of the Israelites as we've been studying together? In all fairness, it was probably a terrifying reality: a massive sea in front of them (remember from earlier weeks that the sea was an image of chaos, destruction and death!) and a massive enemy army behind them! But let's also not forget there was more going on. The Israelites were not left alone or unprotected.

Read Exodus 14:13-14.

02 | We don't have a record of the people's response after hearing Moses' direction. What would your response have been?

The initial response after crying out to God to fight on their behalf was silence. The Israelites surely thought Moses' advice made no sense. However, Moses was leading the people to use silence as a spiritual discipline. Sadly, the idea of solitude and meditation on God's protection, provision and providence is somewhat of a lost practice. But this is exactly what Moses told the people to do: sit silent and watch God protect them and fight on their behalf. If we were the Israelites, we would have probably demanded an explanation for what seemed like such an odd response to such a serious threat.

As we consider our own use of silence in the midst of threats, there can be many benefits. One purpose of silence may be to focus on the simplicity of God's power over all things. Another benefit might be to quiet distractions and interruptions that tempt us to explain away God's protection in our lives. Maybe silence and solitude are ways for us to process and find peace with things that seem so unexplainable in our lives.

What would happen if we practiced the spiritual discipline of silence today by spending focused time meditating on the protection and provision of God in our lives? What if we intentionally remembered to trace God's faithfulness in the past until it helped us feel more safe and secure in the faithful and secure hands of God? The Israelites were aware of this truth through tangible and visible examples but, in that moment, needed to pause and remember.

03 Read Exodus 14:19-20. Who was also with the Israelites? Describe what was happening.

The end of the story is the protection of Israel through God's powerful authority over nature itself. God splits the Red (Reed) Sea in half and creates a passageway of safety for His people to find rescue and deliverance.

However, for the Egyptians, that same passageway would prove to be their burial place. The sea would close in on them, and the army of the most powerful civilization of the known world at the time would be annihilated in a moment.

Remember our earlier discussion about the odd language change from the original Hebrew name for the "Reed Sea" being translated by the authors of the Septuagint as the "Red Sea." It's very possible the translators made a theological decision to name the sea as "Red" to make a heart-stopping connection. Remember in Exodus 1:22 the Nile, also full of reeds, turned red with the blood of innocent children at the hands of the Egyptians. Well, the very sea that the Israelites crossed would turn "red with the blood of their persecutors, the Egyptians."[52] Like the Lord teaches in Deuteronomy 32:35, *"Vengeance is mine, and recompense, for the time when their foot shall slip; for the day of their calamity is at hand, and their doom comes swiftly.'"*

Wrapped up in this story is a greater truth we shouldn't miss. God's protection of His people was set in motion on purpose. Remember, it was God Himself who directed the people of Israel. God led them into the wilderness. God placed them in the most unprotected, defenseless situation, backed into a corner, with the sea (an image of destruction) in front of the people, and Pharaoh and his army behind them (the reality of destruction).

Yet it was God who was at the center of His people, providing protection and orchestrating these events in order to provide an important lesson for them. As one Old Testament scholar has said, "Israel's escape route became a classroom for them, a period of testing in time and space that shaped the people Yahweh was making."[53]

Read Exodus 14:15-18.

04 | Scripture demonstrates that sometimes God allows trials in order to reveal His power. What about this truth is hard to accept?

05 | When you look back at some of the trials from your past, how did some of them become a classroom to shape you in good ways?

The experience at the Red Sea was a formative experience, helping the people of God better understand and live out trust in their Creator.

In the same way, Jesus and His victory over death on the cross is meant to remind us of the unexplainable but necessary sacrificial protection we have received. The more we remember what Jesus has done for us and what it means for us, the more we will be assured of His absolute devotion to protecting us.

Every moment we are with God, we are with His protection whether we realize it or not. And part of that protection, if we will trust Him and stay with Him, is how He will form us and shape us through what we experience.

06 | Read 1 Corinthians 15:49. What is the goal of all of this shaping and forming?

The more we are shaped and formed to be like Jesus, the more we will be confident in God's protection. But even more than being confident, with Jesus we can have unexplainable peace in the process. Philippians 4:7 reminds us of this truth: *"And the peace of God, which surpasses all understanding, will guard your hearts and your minds in Christ Jesus."*

As we conclude today, let's turn to one more story involving another sea. In this New Testament story, found in Mark 4, Jesus is asleep on a boat in the middle of a storm on the Sea of Galilee. This is the type of storm that would put true fear in even the most seasoned sailors. In a moment of desperation, the disciples cry out to Jesus to provide protection for them. Jesus simply wakes up, rebukes the wind and tells the sea to be still.

Simply the PRESENCE OF JESUS and the voice of Jesus *in the midst of the storm* establishes peace. Where Jesus is present, PEACE IS POSSIBLE.

This doesn't mean there won't be storms, trials, tribulations and hardships. Certainly the children of Israel and Moses experienced these. The disciples in the New Testament experienced these. And we will, too. But we are never left alone. He is with us. With Jesus, even when our circumstances don't feel peaceful, we can choose to do things His way and, in doing so, have peace that passes all understanding.

And in the end, if we will just remember to reflect on all the many ways we've seen God move in our past and the peace available to us in the present, we can know we are being protected.

DAY TWENTY-THREE

THE UNLIKELY PROTECTION OF JONAH

Have you ever had a very normal day suddenly take a hard turn?

If anyone could relate to this reality, it was Jonah. I doubt you've ever had the thought that being swallowed by a whale would make you feel protected. But this is exactly what happened with Jonah. What an unlikely "plot twist"! Granted, he certainly didn't see this as a protection. With God, we sometimes get what we don't expect, but we always get what we need. When we read the story of Jonah, that seems to be a repetitive theme.

For example, Jonah is an unlikely candidate for God's mission because the first thing he does is run away. And a whale seems like a very unlikely way for God to show His care, protection and provision of guidance for Jonah. Plus, it seems unlikely that the Ninevites would be spared from the coming judgment due to their sin. All of this reminds us to keep our eyes open for anything that seems unlikely because God shows His presence in unlikely ways; and the book of Jonah really puts this on display.

In Jonah's story, we will learn that the safest place to be is always within the will of God, no matter how unsafe it might look on the surface. And sometimes God protects us from ourselves in ways that are surprising and redirect our path and purpose. For Jonah, God provided some redirection protection through a u-turn that landed him right in the belly of a fish.

The story of Jonah has another very important connection that we may miss at the outset if we don't look intently at the structure, details and purpose of the story: the connection between Jonah and Jesus. First, let's review the historical and cultural situation Jonah found himself in.

Jonah was a prophet from Gath Hepher in Galilee (in Samaria), and prophesied in the northern kingdom of Israel during the reign of Jeroboam. He's one of the 12 minor prophets and one of only a handful that Jesus personally referenced. (Matthew 12:41) But the fact that stands out the most about Jonah is that he's also the only prophet who tried to run from God ... unsuccessfully, we might add.

— A NOTE FROM JOEL

The image of Nineveh being prophesied about here like a *"pool whose waters run away"* (Nahum 2:8) is meant to bring to mind an army that has been defeated and scatters for safety at the end of the battle. Imagine a war movie scene where the soldiers are yelling "retreat!" as they run away. Same idea. The once strong and proud city would be overtaken and scattered in retreat.

The book of Jonah opens with God's command to go to Nineveh and *"call out against it, for their evil has come up before me"* (Jonah 1:2). Nineveh was an immensely important city and at one point became the capital city of the Assyrian Empire. The Ninevites were also enemies of the Israelites. The overwhelming majority of biblical references to Nineveh portray the city as evil (Jonah 1:2) and as a city destined to experience doom. (Nahum 2:8; Nahum 3:7; Zephaniah 2:13)

With Nineveh's reputation for evil and antagonism against the people of God, it's no wonder Jonah is reluctant to declare God's message there. Instead of going to Nineveh like God instructed, Jonah boards a boat in Jopah headed west to Tarshish. This was 2,500 miles in the opposite direction. So this is how we find Jonah on a boat in the middle of the sea. Don't forget what the sea is an image for!

Jonah didn't get very far in his journey before a storm arose.

01 | Read Jonah 1:1-5. Throughout all this chaos, confusion and danger, where is Jonah? What does this tell us about Jonah's state of mind?

Read Jonah 1:6.

This must have been quite a storm if seasoned sailors were afraid and praying to their own gods. Finally, the only response for the sailors is to throw Jonah into the sea. We may expect that the book of Jonah would be one of the shortest Old Testament books, ending at Jonah 1:15-16, but God works in an unlikely way. God saves him, but that protection comes in the form of a great fish or "whale," as it is translated in some versions of the Bible.

Jonah 1:17a says that *"the LORD appointed a great fish to swallow up Jonah."* This is not by chance — this is not random, and this is not arbitrary. God's action always has purpose, and His motivation here is protection.

We may be tempted to think of this massive fish that swallows Jonah as an agent of God's punishment since Jonah disobeyed God. But instead, God appoints the fish as an agent of His divine protection. God still has work for Jonah to do, and He uses the belly of the whale to teach and lead Jonah.

02 | Can you recall a time where God protected you by redirecting your path and placing you in a holding pattern? What did you learn during that time?

We also shouldn't miss the language of the *"belly"* of the whale (Jonah 1:17b). The Hebrew word used here is *mē·'ĕ(h)*. The same word is used in Genesis 15:4 and Ruth 1:11 to describe the "womb of a woman" and is not the expected word *(bĕ·ṭĕn)* that translates as "belly," used later in Jonah 2:1.

Why the change in language? One possible reason may be that we are to see a picture of Jonah entering a time of learning, growing and developing that he may come out of the "womb" a new person.[54] In other words, the imagery may be intended to show us that Jonah went through a type of rebirth or "baptism."

Baptism symbolically represents the process of spiritual death redeemed into spiritual life. In a similar way Jonah enters the water as a doubt-filled and rebellious person, and he is intended to come out of the water a new person filled with faith and living a life of obedience. As we continue to read, we find this isn't exactly what happens with Jonah. Even after he comes out of the water he still has much to learn about God and His ways. Jonah especially needs to learn what it means to be obedient, even when obedience doesn't make sense.

After Jonah's time in the fish, God gives him a second chance to obey.

03 | Read Jonah 3:1-3. What is Jonah's response to the Lord's word this time?

Chapter 3 wraps up quickly after Jonah obeys. The people of Nineveh respond to Jonah's warning that their city will be overthrown. They call a fast and repent, *"from the greatest of them to the least of them"* (Jonah 3:5b). The response is so complete that the king of Nineveh joins his people and calls for a city-wide turning from evil ways. God relents and the Ninevites are saved.

Read Jonah 4:1-3.

In yet another plot twist, Jonah surprises us with his response. One would think Jonah would be relieved that God protected him from the Assyrians (Ninevites). After all, Jonah's warning actually caused them to change! Shouldn't Jonah have been thankful?

04 | Instead, how does Jonah react? Why might Jonah have reacted this way?

Jonah's response isn't all that different from ours at times. It's so satisfying to think of God getting revenge on our enemies. After all, we're told not to exact vengeance but to leave room for God's wrath. (Romans 12:19) It's very possible Jonah was looking forward to watching God pour down His wrath on the Assyrians.

As obedient as Jonah eventually was, his actions and words revealed his true heart and motivations. Here is where we see Jesus, the better Jonah.

Jesus, just like Jonah, found Himself asleep on a boat in the middle of the sea during a great storm. (Matthew 8:23-27) But unlike Jonah, who was thrown out of the boat in order for the storm to cease, Jesus, the greater Jonah, commanded the storm to cease.

Jesus, just like Jonah, found Himself in the darkness of a deep abyss (the grave) for three days. But unlike Jonah, who was sent into the belly of the whale forcefully, Jesus willingly humbled Himself, even to the point of death, and stayed in a tomb for three days. There was no need for an image of death (the sea) because Jesus experienced the very realness of death.

Jesus, just like Jonah, continued His ministry on earth for a period of 40 days (Acts 1:3) after His three days in the tomb. Jesus willingly and joyfully provided forgiveness, salvation and reconciliation for all people from all nations. And He commanded the disciples to go out to the ends of the earth, making disciples from among the nations. (Matthew 28:18-20) But Jonah begrudgingly went to Nineveh, a city of gentile enemies who acted against God and His people, and was disappointed when God relented and forgave them.

Jesus, just like Jonah, was intimately connected to the most unexpected image that would lead to the protection and reconciliation of many. For Jonah, that unexpected image was a fish. For Jesus, that unimaginable image was the cross.

As Andrew Knowles points out: "Jonah gives us one of the Bible's great images of God's power to save. Just as Joseph was rescued from prison to become prime minister, and Daniel was kept safe among lions, Jonah is preserved in the belly of a great fish. These episodes prepare us for their greatest sequel—the resurrection of Jesus from the tomb. Jesus went down into the depths of death and experienced utter loss of God—but was raised as the ultimate proof of salvation."[55]

Today, it is the unlikely symbol of the cross that reminds us of God's love and protection for us. For it was on the cross that Jesus, the Son of God, paid the price for our sins. As we close today, write out a prayer thanking Jesus for protecting us in this way.

THE UNIQUE PROTECTION OF THE TORAH

Joel here. When I was growing up, my mom always gave me her "words of warning." Every time she started to share her wisdom, my natural impulse was to roll my eyes, let my mind drift to some random thought and just endure the "lecture" so I could get myself out of the situation and on with the more important things in my life.

Today, I realize every one of those "words of warning" wasn't a random moment or thought. My mom addressed things she saw in my life that concerned her. She knew if I didn't address the issues at hand, I might go down a dark road that would be very difficult to recover from.

In the Old Testament, God gave us words of warning as well. The first five books of the Bible are called the "Pentateuch," or the "Torah," which can be translated as "the books of the Law." Moses is traditionally believed to be the author of these books and they are key in our understanding of the larger story of Scripture. They are also key in discovering how God has worked in unique ways throughout history in the lives of His people to provide protection. We can also see Jesus in the middle of this protection as well.

Just for clarity with terms, when you see the phrase "Torah," you can know we are discussing the first five books that make up a larger narrative story that includes principles from the Law.

When you read the term "the Law," you will know we are talking specifically about those rules, regulations and commandments that were given to Israel and generally refer to (but aren't limited to) the commandments given in the wilderness of Sinai. (Exodus 19-20) We will come back to all of this shortly, but just tuck this away and hold it close. Laws were added to the Torah and implemented based on the behavior, neglect and/or disobedience of the people of God. This is similar to my mom "lecturing" me based on what she was seeing at the time, to protect me in the future.

— A NOTE FROM LYSA

When we say that "Moses wrote the Torah" we mean that God gave him the Law and the commandments, and Moses faithfully transcribed/presented them to the people.

To summarize, the Torah contains the Law, and laws were added at times based on the downward trajectory of the people of God as a means of protection.

You may be wondering: Why are we even discussing the Torah, and why should we care about the Law? Aren't both of these things obsolete in light of the New Testament? Well, no.

If we ignore or dismiss the Torah and the Law, we will actually miss the fulfillment and completion of both that comes in Jesus, the Messiah. Moses had a purpose in writing the Torah, and it wasn't simply for us to get a list of do's and don'ts. Especially because Moses already knew and prophesied that the Israelites would in fact break the Law. (Deuteronomy 29-34)

So why would Moses take what God gave him and write the Torah and point out the Law at all? What does Moses want us to see, learn and experience? Moses doesn't write the Torah to get us to the Law but to actually help us get through the Law and its brokenness, and finally to the greater promise and fulfillment in the Messiah in the last days.[56]

This is why the Torah and the Law are important to us. When we journey through the Torah, we find it actually leads us to Jesus the Messiah. How does the Torah do this? By serving as a provisional (limited-time) protector of the people of God, the Torah enables us to see Jesus as the embodiment of all that the Torah points to, the "Word" that has become flesh in Christ. (John 1) Jesus makes a startling statement in Matthew 5:17 when He says He didn't come to abolish the law but to fulfill it! This is yet another way we see Jesus in the Old Testament. Jesus fulfills the Torah and all the requirements of the Law.

Today, we'll take a look at three unique ways the Torah serves as **a guardian**, as a **shadow** and as a conduit of **wisdom**. This will help us see God's protection through the Torah.

The Torah as Guardian:

Read Galatians 3:24.

Paul says something truly remarkable: The Law was meant to be our guardian. What does a guardian do but protect, care for and instruct? This means that the Torah should be viewed as a gift of guardianship given to the people of God in order to tutor and train them in the ways to live and love. However, its purpose was for a set period of time. In other words, there was a time and season for the Torah to function, and that season as a guardian and tutor came to completion at the arrival of the Messiah, Jesus.

01 | What are some ways the Law of God serves as a guardian in your life? How has God protected you through His Truth?

The Torah as Shadow:

Read Hebrews 8:1-5.

Part of the Torah and Law includes rules and regulations for the priests and the temple of God. But as the author of Hebrews says, these things (the Torah, Law, priests and temple) were all but a *"copy"* or a *"shadow"* (Hebrews 8:5) intended to point us to the substance behind the shadows. In earlier weeks we talked about how shadows prove that there is a sun. In this instance, again, we can see that the substance behind the shadow (Torah/Law) is none other than Jesus. Without Jesus, the priests, the temple and all the laws would be unfulfilled. They would in a sense be empty. But when we see Jesus as the substance, we can see and experience the full meaning and value of all of these things.

02 | In addition to God's holy Word, the Bible, what things on earth serve as a shadow of heavenly things?

Read Hebrews 8:6-7.

03 | What might the author of Hebrews mean when he says Christ's covenant is *"enacted on better promises"* (v. 6)?

We don't need to guess at what substance is behind the shadows of the Torah because the author of Hebrews says it plainly: Christ is better! And with Christ comes the fullness of the new covenant that illuminates the shadows of the old covenant (as seen in the Torah/Law), bringing completion and fulfillment.

The Torah as Wisdom:

Read 1 Corinthians 9:8-10.

This may seem like an odd text, but Paul is pointing out that the Law was not written for oxen but for us! The way the Law and Torah are to be applied is through the lens of wisdom, which is God-given. In other words, "The Law is an expression of God's great wisdom."[57]

But we may ask: How is this wisdom to be applied and lived out? Well, once again the Torah and Law become very important.

Read Matthew 22:36-40.

04 | Summarize Matthew 22:36-40 in your own words.

What is the heart of the Law? To love God and love others.

We are inundated with ideas of what love looks like. Even our culture suggests that we love others, but that "love" is often motivated by our own desires. There's no shortage of advertisements and reality TV shows that make love look more like a temporary thrill than an unselfish foundation to a lasting relationship.

Our cultural perspective on love may be momentarily exciting but in the end will probably leave us feeling more empty and confused. For Christians, our love for others should be framed first and foremost by our love for God. And it's often through relationships with others where we find opportunities to apply the wisdom of the Bible and demonstrate real love. As we live a life of biblical love, we are fulfilling the heart of the Law.

God's wisdom may be His greatest form of protection for us. If we truly live our lives following the heart of God, we will be led into wisdom. If we keep a humble heart and love others as Christ loves them, we will see that we are living out the very wisdom of God.

Read Psalm 1.

05 | What kind of protection do we see God offering to those who delight in the law of the Lord?

As we wrap up today's study, let's read one more verse about how Jesus points to the Torah:

Read Luke 24:27.

Jesus was literally reading the writings of Moses (the Torah) and showed how all these passages were in fact pointing to Himself. In other words, Jesus was the teacher and tutor who fulfilled all the requirements of the Torah. In doing so, Jesus invites us to look to Him as we live a life reflective of the gospel, marked by love and filled with the wisdom of Jesus.

THE UNCHANGING PROTECTION OF THE DIVINE WARRIOR

Joel here. I heard my son yell, "It's the bat signal!" We happened to be walking through a comic book store and my son saw a replica of the symbol used to light up the night sky of Gotham City letting Batman know his help was needed. I asked my son why he got so excited when he saw that symbol. He responded simply, "Whenever that sign shows up, the bad guys are gonna go to jail and the good guys are gonna be saved."

You see, my son knew instinctively that the bat signal would bring order and justice. Batman would help the innocent people who were being hurt by the "bad guys." Wouldn't it be so nice to have a real-life bat signal today?

When injustice runs rampant and falsehoods are abundant, we may question if there is any protection for the innocent at all.

Throughout the ages, God's people have cried out for God to intervene in unfair situations. Because we are created in the image of God, there is something deep within us that longs for the scales of justice to weigh equal. We want the innocent to be redeemed and those who are guilty to pay amends.

If we've been hurt by injustice, we feel the pain intensely. It makes us feel helpless, frustrated and angry. Sometimes it seems like the guilty go unpunished while we pay the price. This can make us feel like God just doesn't care.

But in our final day of study this week, we hope you will learn that God does not overlook these gross violations. In earlier weeks we discussed issues like injustice and the desire of God to see righteousness and mercy enacted by His people. Today, we will see that the Old Testament clearly points out that God is intently watching the plight of humanity, and He is not a complacent bystander.

When it comes to issues of justice, God reveals Himself as our Divine Warrior. The revelation of God as Divine Warrior in the Old Testament helps us to see the unchanging nature of God and how Jesus is actually the unchanging Divine Warrior in the Old Testament. When we see Jesus as the Divine Warrior in the Old Testament, we can see that Jesus is the same yesterday, today and tomorrow. Jesus is unchanging, and this should bring us great comfort!

Read Isaiah 59:1-16.

In the book of Isaiah we continually see a pattern of injustice. But we also see God's heartache and concern over it. We see these issues come to a head in Isaiah 58-59. Finally, after observing all the injustice (the lack of truth and rampant mockery of righteousness), the Divine Warrior God, Yahweh, would have no more. In Isaiah 59:15-21, the Divine Warrior watches, observes and then acts.

01 | In Isaiah 59:1-16, what issues incite God's anger regarding injustice?

This section of Scripture is often referred to as the "Divine Warrior Hymn."[58] Old Testament scholar John Goldingay reminds us that it is intended to bring to mind the victorious actions of God at creation (remember the image of the sea and chaos and how God brings order) and the deliverance at the Red/Reed Sea, and it also anticipates a future deliverance and victory that will come. It's this last anticipation that we want to hold on to and tuck away.

The specific phrase *"his own arm,"* found in verse 16, is loaded with meaning. The "arm" is a common metaphor used throughout the Old Testament to communicate the power of God in human history. We see this especially in Exodus and Deuteronomy. (Exodus 6:6; Exodus 15:16; Deuteronomy 4:34; Deuteronomy 5:15; Deuteronomy 7:19; Deuteronomy 9:29; Deuteronomy 11:2; Deuteronomy 26:8; Psalm 77:15)[59] Sometimes it's easy to read these descriptions of God and move past them quickly. Let's just slow down a little bit here and remember that another common word used to describe God is "Father."

Joel here. One of the things my boys love to ask me is to show them how strong I am. They love hanging on my arms as I lift them up and down (it's getting increasingly hard to do this as my kids grow!). I think this natural desire of children to see the strength of their dad may be hard-wired into us. We also want to see and know God our Father is strong, and when we come across verses and phrases that show His strength, we are reminded that He truly is all powerful.

This is an important detail to understand. The phrase "his own arm" would have reminded the Israelites that what is about to happen is not new or novel but is evidence of an unchanging and consistent God. It is a continuation of the divine and protective work of God that has been going on for ages.

Sometimes, we need to remind ourselves that the protection of God we desperately desire is secure based on the character of God. God's character is unchanging; therefore, His protection over us is unchanging. Circumstances can sometimes change in ways that disillusion us. People will sometimes change their minds and break their commitments. Even our jobs can sometimes change and cause us to lose our financial security. But God never changes. He has protected and will continue to protect us, fight for what is right and address what is wrong.

When God sees the injustice mentioned in Isaiah 59:15, He prepares to address it in a specific way.

Read Isaiah 59:17.

02 | What does Yahweh put on? Do you see any significance in the order of what God uses to prepare Himself for action?

Of all the things Yahweh puts on, may we focus for a minute on the cloak *(mĕ'îl)*? The Hebrew word translated into "cloak" was a type of clothing used for prophets, (1 Samuel 15:27; Ezra 9:3; Ezra 9:5) priests, (Exodus 28:4; Leviticus 8:7) and kings or royalty. (1 Samuel 18:4; 1 Samuel 24:5; 1 Samuel 24:11; Ezekiel 26:16)

Does that image bring back any memories of earlier days in this study? The imagery causes us to reflect on the Messiah who would be our great Prophet, Priest and King. So, again, the unchanging nature of God is shown in the unchanging consistency of Jesus. As we've seen throughout this study, we see reflections of Jesus through prophets, priests and kings. So how does this comfort us?

Jesus is there in every way we need Him. Just like the prophets, He speaks to us. Just like the priests, He prays and intercedes for us. Just like the kings, He leads and cares for us. But remember, the humans who filled these roles could only do in part what Jesus did in perfection. Therefore, His protection over us in all these ways is also perfectly consistent and unchanging as well. So, when our feelings beg us to believe differently, we can mark this study as the place to return to Truth.

There is another important aspect of the armor that the Divine Warrior puts on. All of the armor emphasizes the significance of the community. The Divine Warrior acts in direct response to the calamity of the community and those who are oppressed.[60]

Read Isaiah 59:18-20.

03 | What will happen when God steps in to enact justice? What does verse 19 tell us about God's motive for repaying those who have turned from His ways?

It is clear the enemies of the Divine Warrior and His people would suffer consequences for their lack of justice, perversion of truth and moral decay. However, who exactly were these enemies? Of all the names that have been mentioned earlier in Isaiah, curiously, we have no mention of Assyria, Egypt, Persia or any other nation that we might expect to find. What could this mean?

Old Testament scholar John Oswalt summarizes the heart of the reason best, saying:

"Yet Israel is still in need of deliverance; it is still defeated. By what? By its inability to live the life of God, to do justice and righteousness (Isaiah 56:1) in the world. Here is the true enemy against which God has come to make war. It is not the Canaanites who are the enemies of God's people, and thus of God; rather, it is the sin that the Canaanites represent. This is the ultimate development of the Divine Warrior motif in the Bible: God comes to destroy the final enemy of what he has created: not the monster Chaos, but the monster Sin."[61]

The fact that the Divine Warrior is dealing with the root issue of sin should cause us to step back and consider who this Divine Warrior figure may be. The clues seem to indicate that the Divine Warrior is in fact the pre-existent and unchanging Warrior-King of heaven and earth, King Jesus. It is finally King Jesus who on the cross vanquishes sin and death. It is King Jesus in Revelation who ushers in the new heavens and new earth, where injustice will have no place and the Kingdom will be set up in righteousness and justice. It very well may be that the Divine Warrior is none other than the God-man, King Jesus.

But something else is also taking place. Today, you and I are being invited into the protection of the Divine Warrior. In Ephesians 6, Paul outlines the armor of God and its protection for us.[62]

Read Ephesians 6:13-17.

04 | List the ways the armor of God protects us.

Notice anything similar? Paul is not referencing some arbitrary armor; rather it seems that he has in mind the very armor of the Divine Warrior, King Jesus. Within this story we find a redemptive reversal. Remember, a redemptive reversal is when God steps in and turns something that was once harmful or hurtful into something good and helpful. It is evidence of God's goodness and power that reminds us that He can redeem the worst of moments and turn it into an ultimate good for us.

A NOTE FROM LYSA

Remember, back in the Old Testament, the story of David, Saul and Goliath. David, as he ventures out to fight Goliath, is given the kingly armor of Saul because Saul doesn't want David to be unarmed. But David puts on the armor and is unable to wear it in comfort. He's not strong enough to wear it. It is not fit for him, and he has not trained for it. In other words, David is not empowered or equipped to wear the armor of the king.

Here in Ephesians 6, you and I, the children of God, are told to wear the armor of the King. However, before we are ever told to wear the armor we are told that we are protected by the guardian Holy Spirit. (Ephesians 1:13-14)

Read Ephesians 6:10-12.

The phrases *"be strong in the Lord"* and *"in the strength of His might"* (v. 10) recall earlier references to the Spirit who raised Christ from the dead and seated Him at the right hand of the Father. (Ephesians 1:19-20) This is the same Spirit that strengthens, equips, empowers and enables us to *"put on"* (Ephesians 6:11), *"take up"* (Ephesians 6:13) and *"take"* (Ephesians 6:17) the armor of the King. In other words we are not like David, who was unable to wear the armor of the king because he was ill equipped and lacked the strength to do so. (1 Samuel 17:38-39) Instead, you and I are protected by the Spirit and equipped to take and put on the armor of the divine King of heaven and earth. It fits us. It is meant for us. It protects us.

Part of putting on the armor that Jesus gives us is living out and upholding justice. Micah 6:8 says it so well:

1. Do justice.
2. Love kindness.
3. Walk humbly with God.

This may feel like a massive task to take on, but maybe it's not as big as we think. What if justice and kindness starts within our homes, schools and workplaces? What if it's the very small things like not cutting corners with our job, volunteering our time, giving resources to organizations that are serving those in the margins of society, and simply (but very importantly) praying for others? When we participate in doing justice, loving kindness and walking humbly with God, we are participating in the life of Jesus and the true and final justice that He will bring when He returns.

05 | Consider an injustice in our world. How does Ephesians 6:10-12 empower you to combat this injustice?

06 | As we close today, how does the unchanging protection of the Divine Warrior specially help you process something you're facing today?

As we wrap up, today let's make an intentional decision to keep our minds fixed on the unchanging nature of Jesus. As we think upon Jesus and the way He acts through love to bring justice and righteousness, kindness and compassion, let's make the decision to join Him in His unchanging ways. Now, let's pray together: *Lord, thank You that You sent Jesus, who deeply understands how hard it can be to process fear inside these frail, hurting, human hearts of ours. Thank You for the hope that Jesus has overcome the world. Now help me overcome what I'm facing today. Thank You for the grace that I don't have to do it perfectly. I just have to make progress. I love You, Lord. In Jesus' Name, Amen.*

CONCLUSION *TO THE STUDY:*

Lysa here. A couple of years ago, I wrote this in my journal: *Jesus told us we would have trouble in this world but then encouraged us to take heart because He'd overcome the world. So why doesn't it feel like He is overcoming the heartbreaking realities in my world?* I was facing so much grief and uncertainty. It seemed some of my favorite parts of my life were unraveling. Nothing was making sense. And just when I thought I could see a light at the end of the tunnel, more hard things hit me.

I got angry at Him.

I wrestled and cried and tried with everything in me to figure things out on my own.

But the more I tried to untangle the mess, the bigger it seemed to get. Nothing was working. Nothing at all was working.

So I knew I had a choice to make. I could either believe that Jesus was with me or get completely swallowed up in all the confusion and pain, believing Jesus had abandoned me. Whatever I chose to focus on is what would be magnified in my life. And I certainly didn't want my problems and pain to get any more magnified. So I started making the choice daily to intentionally declare over my problems that somehow walking through this was going to help me see Jesus more clearly. And it did.

The problems didn't go away. But my courage to face them came back stronger than ever. Knowing I wasn't in this battle alone helped me start believing that Jesus would help me eventually overcome, and I learned so much more about Him in the process. We won't see Him unless we are intentionally seeking and looking.

Now, as we wrap up this study, I think it's time to add a few more lines to that journal entry:

Just because we can't always see Jesus doesn't mean He isn't there.
Just because we aren't hearing Him doesn't mean He's being silent.

I know we've said this in different ways all throughout this study. But maybe you need to read those last two sentences over and over as much as I do.

When the circumstances we face feel crushing,
scary, confusing or truly just impossible to figure out,
how can we know that Jesus really is with us?

After five weeks in this study we hope you can now respond to this question with more assurance of this answer: Because He always has been. And it's more than a promise for the future. It's a reality right now. Jesus is actively with us.

A significant takeaway from this whole study for me has been that if we can see Jesus' presence in the Old Testament then we can have more confidence and assurance He is present in our lives right now, too.

It's surprising how explicit the New Testament authors are about Jesus's presence in the Old Testament:[63]

- The "I Am" in whom Abraham rejoiced was Jesus. (John 8:56-58)
- The Lord who motivated Moses was Christ. (Hebrews 11:26)
- The Redeemer who brought God's people out of Egypt was Jesus. (Jude 5)
- The Rock in the wilderness was Christ. (1 Corinthians 10:4)
- The King of Isaiah's temple vision was the Son. (John 12:40–41)

Jesus is not merely patterned, pointed to and promised in the Old Testament; He is *present*.

Jesus is God's best kept promise. And He hand-delivered that kept promise to earth for us. Look at these instances within the Old Testament that show us God *came down to us*:

- **Genesis 3:8-9**

God came down into the Garden of Eden and sought after Adam and Eve as they hid themselves. God sent them out of Eden not purely punitively but in a way laced with mercy and grace, so they would not live in eternal separation from God.

- **Genesis 11:7**

God came down to observe the people He created in His likeness and image, who had sinned against Him in an act of full-on rebellion. Rather than going out into the world to multiply the image of God and making His name great, as they were commanded, (Genesis 1:28; Genesis 9:1; Genesis 9:7) they decided to reach up into the heavens to make a name for themselves. God diversified their tongues so that they would still spread out and multiply. Another consequence laced with mercy and grace.

- **Genesis 18:20-21**

God came down — He saw and He heard. The outcry against Sodom and Gomorrah was great, and the cries reached God. God wouldn't sit back like an absentee father. No, He investigated the claims, and after His investigation, He acted. And while the city received judgment (justice) in response to overwhelming sin, God still showed mercy and grace by saving Lot and his daughters.

God. Came. Down. And every time, He acted. Through the chaos of rebellion and sin, He continued to act in mercy and grace.

And there's no greater act of God coming down than when He appeared in human history, as recorded in Matthew 1:1.

All the promises of God's presence with us come into fulfillment in the birth of Jesus. And theologically this is referred to as the "incarnation," when God entered human history by taking on human flesh, remaining 100% God and 100% man all at the same time. Theologian Karl Barth said this of Jesus: "This man is the secret of heaven and earth, of the cosmos created by God."[64]

As we reflect on the last five weeks we can remind ourselves that Jesus wasn't absent but that people were looking in all the wrong places.

The incarnation of Christ is a reminder to us all that not a single promise present in the Old Testament was left unfulfilled. C.S. Lewis may have said it best: "The Son of God became a man to enable men to become sons of God."[65] Every single promise of the coming Messiah in the Old Testament came to fruition in the middle of the night in a manger in Bethlehem. Jesus had arrived. He just happened to make His entry in the most unexpected way.

And the same is true in our life right now. He is present. Jesus is never hiding from us. He's waiting to be seen by us.

In the hard places.
In the hurting places.
In the not-yet-healed places.
In the uncertain places.
In the waiting places.
In the celebrating places.
And especially in the everyday places.

We pray you see Jesus.

In the beginning of this study, we shared this truth with you:

Jesus is never absent in the story of the Bible, and He's certainly not absent in any part of our story either.

And we want to remind you of this truth as we bring our time together to a close ... Jesus is our reminder that God always keeps His promises. But if we don't know His promise-filled words, we won't know what to remember. John 8:32 says, *"you will know the truth, and the truth will set you free."* The only truth that sets us free is the truth we know. This is why it's so important to study Scripture because it's the only thing that will lead to freedom.

My opinion will never set me free.
My grace to others will never set me free.
My generosity will never set me free.
My trying to be good enough will never set me free.

If we really want to walk in freedom, we have to remember God is who He says He is and believe with every ounce of faith in our hearts that He really does keep His word. It is the Truth of God that will set us free and keep us from being entrapped by the deceiving lies in our head. Our enemy will sometimes bombard us with harsh comments trying to get us to believe God has forgotten us. But that's when we want you to remember this study. Pull it back down off your shelf and revisit all we've learned during this time together. We promise, we will need to do the very same thing.

So don't stop here. Keep diving into Scripture, learning and looking and seeking more Truth-filled words from God. And when you do, don't forget to look up and see Jesus. Because, from cover to cover, He's there.

He's never been absent. We've never been left alone.

And even better ... He's returning soon. (Revelation 22:12-20) We are held safe in the embrace of a God who promises the comfort of His presence from the garden to glory.

God, thank You that Your Word is so applicable. Lord, help us to remember the Truth we've discovered in Your Word together. We love You so much, God. We make a commitment today to start really paying attention and looking for Jesus in the unexpected places of our lives. In Jesus' Name, Amen.

BONUS RESOURCE: *A Guided Prayer To Receive Salvation*

Hi friend,

When I was in my early 20s, I felt very distant from God. A series of heartbreaking situations in my life made me question His goodness and whether or not He really loved me. But through His divine grace, eventually Truth broke through my cold resistance and brought me to the place where I wanted to accept His love and dedicate my life to Him. The challenge was that I didn't know how to do this and I was too afraid to ask my friends. As I remember struggling through this years ago, I wonder if you might be facing this same struggle, too. Maybe you've had some ups and downs with this whole God thing, but finally you're in a place where you want to give your heart to Him, accept His grace and receive salvation. If that's you, I'd like to invite you to pray this salvation prayer with me today:

> DEAR GOD, thank You for the gifts of grace and forgiveness. Thank You that, in the midst of my sin, You have made a way, through Jesus, to forgive my sin and make me right with You. So today I confess my sinfulness . . . my hard heart . . . my mean thoughts . . . my harsh words . . . my doubt. I believe with all my heart that it was for me — and because of me — that Jesus died. Please forgive me of all my sin. Big sins. Small sins. Past sins. Present sins. And all sins to come. I exchange my sin for Jesus' goodness and holiness. By the shed blood of Jesus, I am now forgiven and free! Thank You that, in this moment, You have sealed me with Your Holy Spirit. I receive this precious gift and trust You will do as You promise and make me a new creation, molding and shaping me from the inside out to be more like You! I celebrate that the old me is gone and the new me is here to stay! I love You and am forever grateful for Your forgiveness and my new life in You. I ask all this in Jesus' name. Amen.

I love you, dear friend. And I'm rejoicing with all of heaven over every decision made to accept God's free gift of salvation. It truly is the sweetest gift we'll ever receive.

Love,

Lysa TerKeurst

"Content taken from Seeing Beautiful Again by Lysa TerKeurst"

END NOTES:

1. In Matthew 1:21-23 the name "Yeshua" means "God will save his people from sins." As NT Scholar Patrick Schreiner says, "The saving from sins is a distinctly priestly task." Additionally, Jesus begins his earthly ministry at 30, the same age priests would begin their priestly duties. (Numbers 4:3, 23, 30, 35, 39, 43, 47; 1 Chronicles 23:3) The Kingship examples are based on the fact that Jesus is called "Son of David," a designation of royalty and kingship. Additionally, all of the Gospels declare that Jesus was the "King of the Jews." (Matthew 27:37; Mark 15:26; Luke 23:38; John 19:19) For more, see: Patrick Schreiner, *The Ascension of Christ: Recovering a Neglected Doctrine* (Lexham Press, 2020).

2. G. K. Beale, *The Temple and the Church's Mission: A Biblical Theology of the Dwelling Place of God,* ed. D. A. Carson, vol. 17, New Studies in Biblical Theology (Downers Grove, IL; England: InterVarsity Press; Apollos, 2004), 81.

3. William Lee Holladay and Ludwig Köhler, *A Concise Hebrew and Aramaic Lexicon of the Old Testament* (Leiden: Brill, 2000), 377.

4. R. Kent Hughes, *Hebrews: An Anchor for the Soul*, vol. 1, Preaching the Word (Wheaton, IL: Crossway Books, 1993), 112.

5. Augustine of Hippo, "The Confessions of St. Augustin," in The Confessions and Letters of St. Augustin with a Sketch of His Life and Work, ed. Philip Schaff, trans. J. G. Pilkington, vol. 1, A Select Library of the Nicene and Post-Nicene Fathers of the Christian Church, First Series (Buffalo, NY: Christian Literature Company, 1886), 45.

6. David Noel Freedman, Helmer Ringgren, and M. P. O'Connor, "יהוה," ed. G. Johannes Botterweck, trans. David E. Green, Theological Dictionary of the Old Testament (Grand Rapids, MI; Cambridge, U.K.: William B. Eerdmans Publishing Company, 1986), 500.

7. Discover the eight major things humanity longs for and how Jesus fulfills all of them for us in *"The Answers to Your Deepest Longings: 40 Days Through the Bible."* Purchase your copy at p31bookstore.com today!

8. See 1 Kings 3:14; 9:4-5; 11:4-6, 31-34, 38; 14:7-8; 15:1-5, 11-15; 2 Kings 14:1-4; 16:1-3; 18:1-3; 22:1-2.

9. This list is an adaption from Michael Wechsler who breaks down the comparison into "shadow" (σκιά) & "substance" (σῶμα). See Michael G. Wechsler, "Shadow and Fulfillment in the Book of Esther," *Bibliotheca Sacra* 154 (1997): 281.

10. Christopher J. H. Wright, *Knowing Jesus Through the Old Testament* (Downers Grove, IL: InterVarsity Press, 2014), 16.

11. Derek Kidner, *Genesis: An Introduction and Commentary,* vol. 1, Tyndale Old Testament Commentaries (Downers Grove, IL: InterVarsity Press, 1967), 75.

12. Douglas Mangum, Miles Custis, and Wendy Widder, *Genesis 1–11*, Lexham Research Commentaries (Bellingham, 2WA: Lexham Press, 2012), Ge 3:1–24.

13. Harry A. Hoffner Jr., *1 & 2 Samuel*, ed. H. Wayne House and William Barrick, Evangelical Exegetical Commentary (Bellingham, WA: Lexham Press, 2015), 1 Sa 2:1.

14. David Tsumura, *The First Book of Samuel,* The New International Commentary on the Old Testament (Grand Rapids, MI: Wm. B. Eerdmans Publishing Co., 2007), 142.

15. R. Bartelmus, "רחב," ed. G. Johannes Botterweck, Helmer Ringgren, and Heinz-Josef Fabry, trans. David E. Green, *Theological Dictionary of the Old Testament* (Grand Rapids, MI; Cambridge, U.K.: William B. Eerdmans Publishing Company, 2004), 431.

16. M. G. Easton, *Easton's Bible Dictionary* (New York: Harper & Brothers, 1893).

17. Peter C. Craigie, Psalms *1–50,* 2nd ed., vol. 19, Word Biblical Commentary (Nashville, TN: Nelson Reference & Electronic, 2004), 68.

18. Kenneth L. Barker, *Micah, Nahum, Habakkuk, Zephaniah,* vol. 20, The New American Commentary (Nashville: Broadman & Holman Publishers, 1999), 95.

19. Hans-Jürgen Zobel, "שבט‎," ed. G. Johannes Botterweck, Helmer Ringgren, and Heinz-Josef Fabry, trans. Douglas W. Stott, *Theological Dictionary of the Old Testament* (Grand Rapids, MI; Cambridge, U.K.: William B. Eerdmans Publishing Company, 2004), 305.

20. JoAnna M. Hoyt, *Amos, Jonah, & Micah,* ed. H. Wayne House and William D. Barrick, Evangelical Exegetical Commentary (Bellingham, WA: Lexham Press, 2018), 727.

21. JoAnna M. Hoyt, Amos, Jonah, & Micah, ed. H. Wayne House and William D. Barrick, Evangelical Exegetical Commentary (Bellingham, WA: Lexham Press, 2018), 732.

22. Cornelius Plantinga Jr., Not the Way It's Supposed to Be: A Breviary of Sin (Grand Rapids, MI; Cambridge, U.K.: William B. Eerdmans Publishing Company, 1995), 32.

23. Chart adapted from: JoAnna M. Hoyt, *Amos, Jonah, & Micah*, ed. H. Wayne House and William D. Barrick, Evangelical Exegetical Commentary (Bellingham, WA: Lexham Press, 2018), 725.

24. Harold G. Stigers, "1879 צדק‎," ed. R. Laird Harris, Gleason L. Archer Jr., and Bruce K. Waltke, *Theological Wordbook of the Old Testament* (Chicago: Moody Press, 1999), 752.

25. William Lee Holladay and Ludwig Köhler, *A Concise Hebrew and Aramaic Lexicon of the Old Testament* (Leiden: Brill, 2000), 221.

26. John Goldingay, *Isaiah for Everyone,* Old Testament for Everyone (Louisville, KY; London: Westminster John Knox Press; Society for Promoting Christian Knowledge, 2015), 43.

27. Both translation taken from John Goldingay.

28. Gary V. Smith, *Isaiah 1–39*, ed. E. Ray Clendenen, The New American Commentary (Nashville: B & H Publishing Group, 2007), 240.

29. John Goldingay, *Isaiah for Everyone,* Old Testament for Everyone (Louisville, KY; London: Westminster John Knox Press; Society for Promoting Christian Knowledge, 2015), 43.

30. David Seal, "Satan," ed. John D. Barry et al., *The Lexham Bible Dictionary* (Bellingham, WA: Lexham Press, 2016).

31. Peter Lau, "Famine," ed. John D. Barry et al., *The Lexham Bible Dictionary* (Bellingham, WA: Lexham Press, 2016).

32. https://enduringword.com/bible-commentary/jeremiah-3/

33. Walter A. Elwell and Philip Wesley Comfort, *Tyndale Bible Dictionary,* Tyndale Reference Library (Wheaton, IL: Tyndale House Publishers, 2001), 1297.

34. M. Görg, "תהוֹ," ed. G. Johannes Botterweck, Helmer Ringgren, and Heinz-Josef Fabry, trans. David E. Green, *Theological Dictionary of the Old Testament* (Grand Rapids, MI; Cambridge, U.K.: William B. Eerdmans Publishing Company, 2006), 565.

35. Peter C. Craigie, *The Book of Deuteronomy,* The New International Commentary on the Old Testament (Grand Rapids, MI: Wm. B. Eerdmans Publishing Co., 1976), 380.

36. Duane L. Christensen, *Deuteronomy* 21:10–34:12, vol. 6B, Word Biblical Commentary (Dallas: Word, Incorporated, 2002), 797.

37. S. R. Driver, *A Critical and Exegetical Commentary on Deuteronomy*, 3rd ed., International Critical Commentary (Edinburgh: T. & T. Clark, 1902), 357.

38. William Lee Holladay and Ludwig Köhler, *A Concise Hebrew and Aramaic Lexicon of the Old Testament* (Leiden: Brill, 2000), 308.

39. JoAnna M. Hoyt, *Amos, Jonah, & Micah*, ed. H. Wayne House and William D. Barrick, Evangelical Exegetical Commentary (Bellingham, WA: Lexham Press, 2018), 728.

40. This quote is from Dr. N.T Wright in his podcast Ask N.T Wright Anything.

41. Richard J. Clifford, The Cosmic Mountain in Canaan and the Old Testament (Wipf and Stock Publishers, 2010), 22.

42. John H. Walton, "The Mesopotamian Background of the Tower of Babel Account and Its Implications," *Bible and Spade* 9, no. 3 (1996): 82.

43. John T. Swann, "Priest," ed. John D. Barry et al., *The Lexham Bible Dictionary* (Bellingham, WA: Lexham Press, 2016).

44. Allen C. Myers, *The Eerdmans Bible Dictionary* (Grand Rapids, MI: Eerdmans, 1987), 487.

45. Dane C. Ortlund, Gentle and Lowly: The Heart of Christ for Sinners and Sufferers (Wheaton, Ill: Crossway, 2020), 57.

46. Dane C. Ortlund, Gentle and Lowly: The Heart of Christ for Sinners and Sufferers (Wheaton, Ill: Crossway, 2020), 57.

47. Flavius Josephus and William Whiston, *The Works of Josephus: Complete and Unabridged* (Peabody: Hendrickson, 1987), 804.

48. Andrew T. Abernethy and Gregory Goswell, God's Messiah in the Old Testament: Expectations of a Coming King (Baker Academic, 2020), 53.

49. Andrew T. Abernethy and Gregory Goswell, God's Messiah in the Old Testament: Expectations of a Coming King (Baker Academic, 2020), 58.

50. Grant R. Osborne, *Matthew*, vol. 1, Zondervan Exegetical Commentary on the New Testament (Grand Rapids, MI: Zondervan, 2010), 229.

51. Thomas R. Schreiner, *Hebrews,* ed. T. Desmond Alexander, Thomas R. Schreiner, and Andreas J. Köstenberger, Evangelical Biblical Theology Commentary (Bellingham, WA: Lexham Press, 2021), 164.

52. Eugene Carpenter, *Exodus,* ed. H. Wayne House and William D. Barrick, vol. 1, Evangelical Exegetical Commentary (Bellingham, WA: Lexham Press, 2012), 500.

53. Eugene Carpenter, *Exodus,* ed. H. Wayne House and William D. Barrick, vol. 1, Evangelical Exegetical Commentary (Bellingham, WA: Lexham Press, 2012), 503.

54. F. Zimmermann, "Problems and Solutions in the Book of Jonah," *Judaism* 40 (1991): 582.

55. Andrew Knowles, The Bible Guide, 1st Augsburg books ed., (Minneapolis, MN: Augsburg, 2001), 370.

56. Seth Postell, Eitan Bar, and Erez Soref, *Reading Moses, Seeing Jesus: How the Torah Fulfills Its Goal in Yeshua* (Bellingham, WA: Weaver Book Company, 2018), 18.

57. Seth Postell, Eitan Bar, and Erez Soref, *Reading Moses, Seeing Jesus: How the Torah Fulfills Its Goal in Yeshu*a (Bellingham, WA: Weaver Book Company, 2018), 94.

58. John Goldingay, *A Critical and Exegetical Commentary on Isaiah* 56–66, ed. G. I. Davies and C. M. Tuckett, International Critical Commentary (London; New Delhi; New York; Sydney: Bloomsbury, 2014), 221.

59. Andrew T. Abernethy, *The Book of Isaiah and God's Kingdom: A Thematic—Theological Approach*, ed. D. A. Carson, vol. 40, New Studies in Biblical Theology (Downers Grove, IL; London: Apollos; InterVarsity Press, 2016), 90.

60. John Goldingay, *A Critical and Exegetical Commentary on Isaiah* 56–66, ed. G. I. Davies and C. M. Tuckett, International Critical Commentary (London; New Delhi; New York; Sydney: Bloomsbury, 2014), 221.

61. John N. Oswalt, *The Book of Isaiah, Chapters 40–66,* The New International Commentary on the Old Testament (Grand Rapids, MI: Wm. B. Eerdmans Publishing Co., 1998), 527.

62. John N. Oswalt, *The Book of Isaiah, Chapters 40–66,* The New International Commentary on the Old Testament (Grand Rapids, MI: Wm. B. Eerdmans Publishing Co., 1998), 528.

63. https://www.desiringgod.org/articles/where-is-jesus-in-the-old-testament

64. Karl Barth, *Church Dogmatics III/1, The Doctrine of Creation, Part 1*, ed. G. W. Bromiley and T. F. Torrance (Edinburgh: T&T Clark, 1958), p. 21.

65. C. S. Lewis, *Mere Christianity* (New York: HarperOne, 2001), 178.

THANK YOU TO THESE GENEROUS DONORS
who made it *possible* for this study to reach the hands and hearts of *many*.

Passionate about sharing God's Word? Email givetruth@proverbs31.org and we'll be in touch about how you can support our next ministry initiative!

"In memory of Jean Nelson, a *faithful* friend, encourager and *powerful* prayer warrior. Although missed by many, she now *radiates* love and joy from the heavenly realms."

DEANNA AND GREG MILLER

"For the woman who needs a *reminder* that she is not alone. She is seen. She is wanted. And, most of all, she is loved. *Always.*"

LAUREN AND MATT FILBECK

"In honor of my mother, Connie Harding, who *changed* my life the second she CHOSE me. She showed me the *love* of Christ and has loved me *without* measure." 2 Corinthians 2:5-7

BECKY RICHARDSON

"In honor of Aunt Mary, a strong, *independent* woman who introduced me to God and brought me to church as a child. The seed you planted *continues* to grow and spread."

MELISSA COTE

"In remembrance of my parents, John and Jenny, who *faithfully* demonstrated both stewardship and the importance of *supporting* those who spread the gospel."

CYNTHIA AND RANDY FOLSOM

"In honor of Daisy Guillotte: a *devoted*, Christian wife for 65 years and a *loving* mother who (with Dad, Nelson) taught her six children what *unconditional*, everlasting, Christian love looks like."

CAROL AND RIC OBENBERGER

"In honor of my Galax, VA, spiritual *warriors* and Bible studies ladies: Renee, Megan, Leah, Jaime, Jessica, Ashley, Sarah. You have taught me *so* much. Thank you." Proverbs 27:17

LISA ADAMS

"In loving memory of our mother and grandmother, Joyce Carver Kindred. You were *always* present and participated in not only our lives but all who crossed your path."

JERRI CARVER

"In memory of my *beloved* uncle, Glenn Wipf. For me, he was the hands *and* feet of Jesus." Psalm 22:10

NAOMI THIESSEN

"To the Monday Bible Study girls: Thank you for challenges, *inspiration* and most of all a *love* of the Lord, leading all of us closer in relationship with Him. With love,"

JO BOBB

"I pray that *discovering* Christ in the Old Testament helps you internalize that, from the very beginning, God has been redeeming us for a *personal* relationship with Him."

CATHY CHUNG

"In *honor* of my grandmothers, Thelma Nordahl and Evelyn Wilcox, whose prayers laid the *foundation* of my faith."

JOAN SCHAFER

WHAT IF OUR TIME
WITH GOD HAS *LITTLE* TO
DO WITH QUIETING
EVERYTHING **AROUND US,**

AND INSTEAD HAS
EVERYTHING TO DO WITH
MAKING AN APPOINTMENT
TO *QUIET* THINGS **WITHIN US?**